The
Magnificent
Three

NICKY CRUZ

with Charles Paul Conn

The
Magnificent
Three

Fleming H. Revell Company
Old Tappan, New Jersey

Library of Congress Cataloging in Publication Data

Cruz, Nicky.
    The Magnificent Three.

    1. Trinity. 2. Cruz, Nicky. I. Conn, Charles
Paul, joint author. II. Title.
BT113.C78   231   76-4574
ISBN 0-8007-0788-5

Contents

A Word From the Publishers

"Dynamite! A real turn-on!" said one of our editors. And we knew we had something special. We felt obliged to let you know that reading about the way Nicky's life and the lives of those around him have been dramatically changed by the separate ministries of the Father, Son, and Holy Spirit can open up new understanding for the possibilities in YOUR life.

Nicky lays it on you with his hard-hitting straight talk. You are there with him—in the tenement, in the jail. You follow him in using what he learns in his ministry—in his home and in his pulpit.

This man has seen life from both sides: as a sinner and as one saved; as a bitter young man and as a mature father of four children; as a gang leader for hoods in the ghetto and as a full-time evangelist. Nicky brings the three faces of God into focus for us. This street fighter turned man of God shows a penetrating—sometimes withering—insight into the contemporary church and the Christian walk.

If you seek a heavy, theological treatise on the Trinity, this is not for you. For here is warmth and compassion; here is personal understanding; here is something you can get hold of for yourself.

We are proud to be a part of Nicky Cruz's continuing ministry.

The Publishers

Foreword

When I married Nicky fourteen years ago, we dedicated our marriage and our lives together to the work of the Lord.

What can I say about the private Nicky Cruz? In his many roles as husband, father, evangelist, counselor, and friend, I see a man who cares enough to be involved with people—at whatever cost, time, or personal sacrifice. Nicky loves people and he loves Jesus, and that is a powerful combination in a man!

Of course, in the last several years, Nicky has traveled so much, we haven't been together as much as we both would like to be, and I have seen times when Nicky has battled against the loneliness that goes with traveling alone so much. In the same day addressing a

crowd of thousands of people, and yet not having a personal contact within the same day—that can blow a man's
mind!

During these times of traveling, what about the
children? They have asked, Why is our daddy never with
us on weekends, when all the other families around have
their daddies home? I have explained that we are sharing
our daddy with those who don't know how wonderful
it is to love Jesus. They have learned what that means,
and they are satisfied with that answer because they
too love Jesus in a personal way.

What about me? The best I can describe my own
experience is to say that as we face our own weakness
we find strength, not only in the Lord, but within ourselves. It is a great privilege to be a part of Nicky's ministry, through his crusades, kids' centers, and books.
I know that for him to have the time to do all that he
does, I have to do more than my share around the home
base. I am grateful to be able to do this for the Gospel,
and for the man I love.

I have enjoyed sharing ideas with Nicky as he has
worked on this book. It is a special book. It talks about
that strong, man's love for the Father, Saviour, and Holy
Spirit that has marked Nicky's life since he first became
a Christian. Its message comes straight from his heart
and I know that you will be inspired by it.

GLORIA CRUZ

1

The Three Faces
of God

When I first became a Christian, I knew nothing about anything. So far as the things of God were concerned, I was a totally ignorant man. I knew nothing.

But Jesus reached me despite my ignorance of Him. I was a filthy, sinful, murdering street fighter, a criminal, full of bitterness and hatred. But a skinny preacher stood on a street corner one day and told me that Jesus loved me. That's all. He just told me that Jesus loved me and that He had suffered and died for me to show His love.

That preacher's name was Dave Wilkerson, and it was a good thing he told me what he did. Many preachers would have looked at my sins and my rotten life and told me I was going to hell. I'm glad Dave Wilkerson didn't tell me that, because if he had said that to me, then, he would have been dead to me. If he had said, "You are going to hell, Nicky Cruz," I could have lashed out at him as I had at everyone else who tried to reach me. I was miserable enough already. I was in a kind of hell already. I didn't need someone to come along and tell me what a bad dude I was, what a hot hell I was heading for. If Wilkerson had told me I was going to hell, I would have planned his funeral.

But he did not tell me that. He told me instead that Jesus loved me. It was so simple. No theology or philosophy or mysterious, deep things of the church. No intellectual stuff. Just, "Jesus loves you, Nicky." I couldn't get mad at that! No way to be confused by that. It touched the deepest part of me, and it broke me, and made me want the love of this Jesus who loved me even when I was so evil and so unloveable.

So I came to Jesus because I knew He loved me, and still I didn't know anything about God.

Very soon I began to discover how complicated the things of God can be. At least to me they seemed complicated. Terribly complicated. It had been simple enough to believe that Jesus loved me, and to confess my sins to Him. But then I began to study the Bible, to hear different preachers preach, to listen to discussions of theology. I was like a little baby who is hungry, sitting at a table with adults who are eating steak and green beans and baked potatoes. The food was there, but I had to grow before I could eat it. I had some catching up to do. For many years I had been like an animal in the streets, and I had no background in church or Sunday school to rely on.

So the Christian people in New York who had brought me to Jesus began to teach me the things of God. They were patient and good to me. They brought me along slowly, so I could digest what I was learning. But still I found many things confusing.

Of all the mysteries of the Bible, none was so mysterious as the concept of the Trinity. I just could not understand it. Three gods? No. One God? Yes. But with three names, three faces, three personalities? Yes, something like that. Three gods in one, then? No, not quite. *One God in three persons,* they explained it to me. Father, Son, Holy Spirit—all one, yet separate; all one God, but somehow different.

I didn't understand it. I believed it was true, though at first only because I had such great confidence in those who taught it to me. Then later I believed it was true because I saw it to be true in the Bible. I saw, over and over, the clear teaching in Scripture of these three faces of God. So I believed it, but I still did not understand it. And, since I could not understand it, I wondered why God made it all so confusing!

Why have three persons, I thought, when it confuses me so much? It seemed to me such a totally unnecessary complication. Why couldn't God just be God? Then I could understand Him. This "Trinity" business I accepted by faith, but I could not relate to it at all.

Now, many years later, much has changed in my life. I am a different man from the Nicky Cruz of

The Cross and the Switchblade. I am in many ways a typical middle-class American suburbanite. I live in a comfortable house on a nice, tree-lined street in Raleigh, North Carolina. I have a wife, and am the father of four daughters, one of them a teenager. I have to think about all the things that most men in their mid-thirties think about: new tires for the car, what kind of schools the kids will go to, finding time to be alone with my wife, Gloria, what to do about the upkeep of our home, and all that. That is a long way from Brooklyn, the Mau Mau gang, and the days of pistols and shotguns, leather jackets, and gang fights in the streets and subways of New York.

For the past thirteen years I have been an evangelist, crisscrossing the country and traveling around the world in crusades and evangelistic services. I work with churches of every type, from Catholic to Pentecostal, large and small. I preach in sanctuaries, prisons, ball parks and stadiums, auditoriums, high-school assemblies, and even still occasionally on the streets. I talk with thousands of people every year, people who know God and people who do not. I believe that I am in touch with the church, with those who are still seeking God, and those who are not seeking at all.

Something has happened in me over those years of ministry that I would never have predicted. Something has emerged in my walk with God that has become the most important element of my discipleship. It has become the thing that sustains me, that feeds me, that keeps me steady when I am shaky. *I have come to see*

God, to know Him, to relate to Him as Three-in-One,
God as Trinity, God as Father, Saviour, and Holy Spirit.
God has given to me over the years a vision of Himself
as Three-in-One, and the ability to relate to God in that
way is the single most important fact of my Christian
growth.

I am not talking about theology. What I am de-
scribing is something different from merely believing in
the doctrine of the Trinity. I have always believed in
the doctrine of the Trinity but I had never experienced
God personally as Three-in-One. It was at first merely a
doctrine in which I believed, but now it has become a
truth of everyday life. God has developed in me a sense
of the separate relationships which I can have with
Father, Saviour, and Holy Spirit. He has shown me the
strength that comes from those separate relationships,
the power for living that comes from the three faces of
God. He has taught me to feed off the Trinity for my
daily sustenance, rather than just having some vague
feeling that the Trinity is somehow true.

Over the years, God has answered that question that
puzzled me so early in my Christian walk: the question
of why God confuses us with this concept of His three-
person nature. Now I understand. I understand that
God is so much more to me as Three-in-One than He
could ever be in any other way. I know now how much
easier it is for me to relate to Him in that day-to-day
way because He is three.

It would be a serious error to think of the Magnificent Three as three gods. There are not three gods;

there is one God. But He comes to me in three forms, in three persons, and it is only by knowing these three separately that I can receive all of what God wants to give me. Since God is a God of three persons, it is for a purpose, and we cheat ourselves to ignore His three-in-one nature just because we cannot understand it completely.

In this book I want to tell you about the God whom I serve. I like to think of God as the Magnificent Three. That concept may not strike some as being attractive, or even theologically appropriate. But it is the way that I see God, and I want to share it with you. This is not a doctrinal treatise on the Trinity. It is not a theological statement. I am not capable of that. It is a personal statement, a testimony, a simple sharing of how God the Magnificent Three lives in my life every day.

I want to tell you about the magnificent Jesus Christ of Nazareth, who is here with me right now in this room. I want to tell you how He heals me, how He pours the ointment of heaven into my wounds, how He loves me and kisses my hurting pain away.

I want to tell you about the magnificent Father, who is so strong that with Him I am always a helpless little baby. I want to share how He protects me and provides for me, and how He cracks me over the head when I get out of line and spanks me until I jump back onto His lap and embrace Him again.

I want to tell you about the magnificent Holy Spirit, the strange, moving presence that sees what I cannot see and reveals it to me, even when it is my own sin. I want to talk about the Holy Spirit, who opens me up so that miracles can have a chance to happen in my life just when I need them the most.

What is God to me? He is One; but He is Three. He is Father, Saviour, Holy Spirit. He is God the Magnificent Three, same yet different, separate yet unified. Logically, rationally, I still do not understand it with my human mind. But I experience it every day!

THE
MAGNIFICENT
SAVIOUR

2

Stand Up, Jesus!

Stand up, Jesus!

Stand up and let them see You! Let these proud, cocky people see You. Stand up and let them see what You are really like!

Oh, Jesus, if just once You would walk into our world as You did in the old days, and show Yourself to the people as You did then! They don't know who You are or what You are really like, Jesus. They have You pictured all wrong, these modern men, so wrapped up in their own puny power, their own silly machismo. They think they have rejected Jesus and they have never seen the real Jesus. Stand up, Jesus, and let them see You, Your muscles and Your tears, Your force and Your power and the aching of Your innards with the terrible hurt You feel for their sins.

They've got You figured all wrong, Lord. Stand up when men preach and when men write and let them see the real Jesus! Stand up in front of them when they hear Your name and show them Your raw, driving power and Your clean, strong love. Show them what a God-plus-man is really like, Lord!

They need someone to respect, to admire, someone to take their breath away, to leave them openmouthed and awestruck, to compel them to follow by the sheer force of his presence. All they have is Super Fly and the Six Million Dollar Man. All they have is football players and millionaires and gangsters, Lord. They need to see a God-man, just once to see a God-man. They need someone to worship, Lord!

They think they already know You, but they don't. They know a counterfeit, phony, cardboard Jesus! They know a nursery-rhyme character, a pitiful, wincing Jesus left over from old Sunday-school lessons.

They know a Jesus with beautiful curly hair, a Jesus fresh from the beauty parlor. No way, Lord!

They know a Jesus of weak, prissy gestures, of pasty-white skin and delicate features. No way, Lord!

They know a Jesus with weakness and pretty table manners. How did they get it so wrong, Lord? How did they miss the scars on Your hands, the power in Your stride, Your strong, masculine way of moving and talking? How could they believe those unreal, faded pictures that look down from the stained glass and peek out shyly from the leaflets?

Stand up, Lord, and let them see the real Jesus! Let them hear that roar of Your voice, that fearsome bellow as the money tables crash and splinter on the Temple floor. Let them hear the terrible, sick sound of the hammer on the spike that tears the flesh, Lord! Let them see the flash and the fire as You preach and Your enemies tremble! Let them see You break the bread and the boiled eggs and pull the fish apart with Your hands and eat when You are hungry, really hungry, Lord, and see if they don't know You better. Let them see You grunt and strain against the cross-saw until the board finally begins to give and the carpenter's shop hums with the sound of metal against wood. Let them see You tired and sagging, eyes bloodshot with exhaustion and the glare of the hot sun, after a day of walking and healing and preaching. Let them see You all charged up and angry, backed into a corner by the scribes and Pharisees, fighting Your way out with words cracking like rifle shots over their heads.

No way, Jesus, could they see You as You really are and not love You, not worship, not want to touch You!

I remember when I saw the real Jesus for the first time. Suddenly I saw You as You really were. I saw that You were human, just like me—that You were strong and full of passion and emotion and volatile energy; I saw that You were the underdog, kicked and beaten and killed for something You didn't do. I saw that You had courage, You had guts, You had something I couldn't describe, something I had never seen before, something incredibly strong and tender all at the same time. I saw that You had the power to squash me like a bug, and instead You poured out Your blood to save me, to love me, to heal my aching heart.

And when I saw the real Jesus, there was nothing to do but fall on my face and embrace You. Nothing to do but love that kind of Jesus who is God and who is man.

This is a wicked world, Lord, full of people who reject You and have never seen You. They sit over martinis and milk shakes and afternoon coffee and smugly think they are too big, too important, too intelligent, too masculine to love Jesus. They need You, Jesus, and they don't even know what You are. Stand up before them like You did to me, Lord! Bust them over the head with a vision of the real Jesus!

3

Chico

Chico was a junkie. A drug addict. He was tall and handsome in a rough sort of way, with a strong, good-looking face. But he was a junkie. He was what a judge might call the garbage of society.

Gloria brought Chico into the drug-treatment center in New York one day while I was working there. She had found him outside the center, bent over with sickness, retching and vomiting on the sidewalk. He was on the streets again after a stretch in prison. On his face you could see the scars of sin. He was sick with two kinds of sickness—the hatred and bitterness of sin and the sickness of a diseased body. We took him in.

From the very first day, Chico gave us nothing but trouble. He was a bad dude. He was locked into him-

self, living with mental torture that hurt him and
clawed at his insides, and occasionally, without warning,
burst out in violence and fighting. Chico never shared,
never talked. He was into himself, tight and hostile.
And sometimes his depression turned dangerous and
Chico lashed out at those of us who tried to help him.

Many people today would say that Chico was demon-
possessed. I don't believe he was. He was a hurting man,
that's all. It didn't take a demon inside Chico to make
him act the way he did. He had a deep, hurting pain
inside, and it made him a miserable and dangerous man.
I grew to love him in Christ. To me I guess Chico was a
challenge. Some of the people at the center wanted to
kick him out and bar him from the center because of
all the trouble he caused. But I grew to love him more
and more in Christ, and I began to pray and fast for him.

One Saturday night I was sitting at the desk in my
study, working on a magazine article I was trying to
write. It was hard work and I was deep in thought.
Chico shoved the door open and walked in. No knock,
no nothing. He just walked straight in. He didn't know
what etiquette was. He didn't say, "Excuse me" or "I'm
sorry" or anything at all; he just shoved through the
door and there he stood, looking down at me with that
hard way of looking that he had.

When he finally spoke, it was short and abrupt.
"Man, I know you wanna know who I am. I'm hurting.
I want to talk to you."

I was stunned, didn't know just how to respond to

such a strange, hard message. "Come on in, Chico," I said. "Sit down."

He spoke without sitting. "Do you know anything about suffering, man?"

"Well, sure, I think I do," I told him. "I was hurting, too, Chico. I grew up with hatred and bitterness against people, against God. I know what it is to have problems, too."

"But you haven't suffered as much as I have," he interrupted.

"Maybe you're right. I don't doubt it, Chico." I was grasping for the right thing to say. I could tell that something strong was going on inside Chico, and I struggled to know how to answer him. "I don't doubt that you've suffered more than me. Maybe you have, maybe not. But what difference does it make? There are people who are suffering more than you right now, too."

He blurted, "I want you to do something. I want you to come with me tomorrow, to take me to a place."

"Chico," I said, "you're not gonna come in here like a crazy man and *tell* me. You say 'please' if you want something." I was getting a little hot at him, and it was showing.

He came back at me hard and cold. "Man, I don't say *please* to nobody. If you wanna come without making me say *please,* I want you to come with me tomorrow. I want you to take me to a place."

"All right," I said after a moment. "If you wanna talk like that, okay. You want me to go, I'll go. You don't know anything about manners, Chico, but okay,

I'll go. If it's going to help you, I'll do anything that will help you. What time do you want me to go?"

"Nine o'clock."

"But Chico, I've got to go to church!"

"To ———— with the church, man!" That sudden, black anger was there, as I had seen it before. His face was a mixture of pain and hostility. "I'm telling you if you wanna come, if you wanna know who I am, why I'm hurting, I'm saying you come with me at nine."

"Okay, okay, don't get uptight," I answered. "Tomorrow at nine I'll be ready."

The next day we left the center together in a van. As we drove, I thought, What is this guy trying to do? What is his game? Is he trying to show me up, make me look bad? Is he trying me out or what?

We stopped at a run-down old building. As we pulled up to the curb, the thought suddenly hit me: He respects me, but he doesn't show it. Maybe he doesn't even know it yet, but he respects me and trusts me, and he knows that I want to help him. He knows I am the only one he can walk in there and talk to like that. And it has nothing to do with the street. Somehow he can tell I love him, and he respects that.

We entered the building and climbed to the third floor. The whole place smelled so bad! Terrible! All kinds of garbage and waste were strewn everywhere. What are we doing here? I wondered. Is he going to find someone to give him a fix or what?

He stopped at a door and pushed it open without knocking. As the door swung open, I felt like vomiting, the smell that came from the room was so bad. Chico began to call somebody's name.

"Carmen. Carmen."

He called softly, almost gently, and somehow it sounded so unlike Chico that in a strange way it was moving to hear him call like that.

"Carmen. Carmen." Nobody answered.

We went in. The smell and the sight of filth and waste was overpowering. I looked into the darkness and saw two little boys, both obviously retarded. They were filthy and scared to death, lying huddled together on a dirty cloth on the floor.

We pushed open a door leading into a second room and there was Chico's sister. She was huddled in a corner, fear in her face, looking wildly at us, like a savage, a beast, a cornered animal in that small, dirty room. She was holding a baby tightly in her arms, and flies crawled all over her and the baby. The baby's diapers had not been changed in days. She clutched the baby more closely when she saw us, afraid we were going to take it away from her. She screamed at us not to come closer, swearing that she would kill herself before she would give up the baby. She cried and threw her head wildly and clutched the baby to herself.

Chico started to cry, caught himself, and yelled, "Please don't, Carmen, please don't be afraid! We are your friends. This is my friend."

I edged closer to her. "Give me the baby. For God's sake give me the baby. I'm going to get you out of here. You need to go to the hospital. The baby needs to go to the hospital. We've got to get him some food and medicine. Carmen, please, just give me the baby!"

I was crying myself now as I pleaded with her, "Carmen, Chico brought me here to help. In the name of Jesus, give me the baby!" She hesitated, looked at me, then handed the baby over. It stank, and the smell and the mess was soon all over my clothes and my hands. I got the baby and Carmen into the van and to a hospital, along with the two boys. I called a social-service agency that I knew about, and they promised to help.

Chico and I drove through the empty Sunday-morning streets back toward the center in dead silence. I was broken. I was really broken. It was quiet in that car, and every time I looked over at Chico, I was more broken and more ashamed. When we got to the center I turned to him and ended the silence. "Chico," I said, "I guess you're right. I didn't know. Chico, I want you to come with me right now to the center, and I want you to go to the chapel with me where we can talk. I want you to talk to me, man, I want you to tell me everything that is inside you. Something is eating you on the inside, and you showed me some of what it is and I want you to get it all out.

"Chico," I said, and I couldn't stop the tears, "Chico, I want to tell you, man, that I love you in Christ, and I want to see a miracle in your life. I know right now you don't believe it, but you're gonna see it with your own eyes. I claim you, brother, in the name of Jesus." I looked at him and he sat and looked straight back at me without flinching or batting an eye, without a trace of emotion or a hint that he was even hearing me. "I don't know how long it's gonna take, Chico, but I'm gonna pray you into the kingdom of heaven."

That day Chico started to open up to me. He told me things that broke my heart and hurt me inside because the hurt he felt was so strong and so plain to see.

"You know," Chico told me a few days later, "one thing I always loved was my mother. I hated for her to suffer. The last time I got out of prison and went back out onto the streets, I went to see her. I had hurt her so many times so bad, and I knew how she had suffered. When I went to see her the last time, she grabbed a butcher knife from the kitchen cabinet and screamed at me, 'Chico, why don't you kill me? Why don't you open my chest and eat my heart right out! I can no longer take it. I can no longer live and see you the way you are. I can no longer stand to see you like an animal, locked up in a cage, turning bitter and mean. The next time you send yourself to prison I'm going to kill myself!'

"And I said to her, 'Oh, no, you won't, Mother. You love me too much to leave me. You have to take me the way I am, because there's no other choice for you, Mother.' "

Chico got busted soon after that on another narcotics charge. They sent him to a prison in upstate New York. Three weeks later, his mother went out and bought a gallon of gasoline for twenty-five cents, dumped it over her clothes and body, and burned herself to death.

At the prison, officials received word of the death of

Chico's mother and were afraid to tell him. A week went by and he received no letter from his mother. Somehow he knew, he didn't have to be told, he just knew. He tasted it in his mouth, he felt it in the pit of his stomach. Somehow he knew that something was wrong with his mother. He demanded to know, so finally they told him. And like a wild animal, he went berserk in his cage. He tore the cell to pieces, tore the toilet and sink from the wall and smashed them to bits, then collapsed like a broken doll when his rage and energy were spent.

A year later he was released, and when he got back on the street, more news awaited him. A brother, also a junkie, had become involved in organized crime, wound up on the short end of a double cross, and was found dead, hung by the neck with a wire rope. Another brother was an addict whose mind was gone, wasted, totally blown by drugs, and now he was a patient in a mental hospital. And his sister was the terribly retarded girl I had seen, who had been abused many times over, and had become, hardly knowing how or why, the "mother" of three children in that stinking third-floor apartment.

As the days passed and I learned more about Chico, I wondered to myself, How in the world is this guy still in his right mind? No wonder he is so hard! He doesn't have any more pain to feel or any more emotions to feel with. He has no more tears to shed. If I threw an atomic bomb at his feet, he wouldn't feel anything because he doesn't have any more feeling left. I prayed and fasted and prayed some more for Chico. I claimed him for

Jesus. But sometimes I wondered if Jesus could ever break through to him.

One day we were having chapel service at the center, and I was supposed to preach. Sometimes you feel like you want to preach a powerful, dynamic sermon. Dynamite! Bam! Pow! Hitting the pulpit, praise the Lord, *hallelujah,* and all that. In those days I almost always preached that way. I felt that we hadn't had service unless I preached that kind of sermon. But on this particular day I felt it wasn't the thing to do. I said to the people, "I don't think God wants me to preach some big fancy sermon today. Let's just sit quietly and sing a chorus." So I led the group in singing "Oh, How I Love Jesus." We sang the chorus over and over. Chico was there that day. He stood in the back of the chapel, eyes full of bitterness, looking at everybody without moving a muscle, not saying a word, nothing moving but his eyes.

We sang "Oh, How I Love Jesus" nine or ten times, and I felt the presence of Jesus so strongly in that little chapel. "Why don't you all just close your eyes," I told the group. "Just close your eyes and see the love of Jesus. Just see the love of Jesus." And we all did. The singing stopped and we all stood quietly, eyes closed, with everyone but Chico — I thought — reflecting on the love of Jesus.

Suddenly I heard a loud, banging racket from the back of the room. I didn't look up. I kept praying as the Spirit moved. And when I opened my eyes, there he was! There was Chico, on his knees in front of me, with tears pouring down his face, broken and pleading. All the fight and fire were gone from his eyes as he looked up at me and said, "Nicky, I feel Jesus here. I want Jesus now, Nicky, now, I want Him to help me with this hurting I have inside."

I just fell on my knees and hugged that man, pulled him tight to my chest and hugged him strong and hard and prayed to the God who loved us both. I prayed for a miracle that day—I prayed for a complete change in Chico. And there, as the pain of an incredibly tortured life poured from his heart, Chico confessed his sins and came to know Jesus as Saviour and Lord. He later went on to Bible school, and today is a strong Christian, married and stable, living for Jesus every day.

Do you see the miracle of what happened there that day? Chico finally saw the real Jesus! He finally saw the Jesus of the Bible—not one of the phony Jesuses that men have made, but the real Jesus, the God-man who is strong and gentle, powerful and tender, who loves the sinner while He hates the sin. Chico had seen all the other Jesuses before, but this day he saw the real Jesus.

He had seen the Jesus of church tradition, the Jesus with a sickly smile and one hand weakly raised in a Boy Scout salute. Do you think that did anything for Chico? Did that Jesus do anything for all the poison in his heart and in his head? No way!

Chico had seen the Jesus of the Christmas cards, the plump baby in a crib with jewel-covered gifts lying in the hay and a yellow halo hovering overhead. Do you think that spoke to Chico's pain, gave him something to grab for, to cling to while his life was being sucked from him by drugs and sickness? No way!

Chico had seen many Jesuses in his life, all of them unreal, incomplete Jesuses: Jesus from Hollywood, Jesus on a greeting card, Jesus carved in the wood of a Catholic altar. So Chico thought he knew all about Jesus, and he thought Jesus was a big bunch of baloney, and he thought that there was no way Jesus çould help him. Chico thought he knew all about Jesus. But he didn't. Chico thought he had rejected Jesus long ago. But he hadn't. He had rejected only those puny, watered-down forms of man-made Jesus. But finally the real Jesus stood up in Chico's life, and somehow, by some miracle, Chico was able to look past all the phony Jesuses and see the real Son of God, Jesus Christ of Nazareth, King and Creator of the Universe, Saviour of all men! Chico saw that Jesus, the Jesus of the soft heart and the tough skin, the Jesus who hugged little children to His bosom and ripped the Pharisees until the skies fairly crackled, the Jesus of raw, frightening power and gentle, tender love.

Chico saw the Jesus of the cross, and for the first time in his life, Chico could feel the pain of those nails tearing flesh, that hot Judean sun beating down, the sharp, stinging hurt of the crown of thorns, the sickening feeling of life oozing out through a jagged spear wound in His side. Chico saw the Jesus of the Bible, and for the first time he could sense the possibility, maybe just a small hope at first, but at least a possibility, of being embraced and loved by this man, this God, this powerful, strange, compelling Jesus Christ.

Chico finally saw Jesus as He really is, and Chico came to Him like a piece of metal drawn to a magnet.

Were we surprised? We shouldn't have been. If we believed the Bible, we could have known it would happen. Jesus himself said it: "If I be lifted up . . . [I] will draw all men unto me" (John 12:32). That is God's word, and it will happen every time! Every time the real Jesus—not a man-made version, distorted and twisted to suit our own desires, but the real Jesus—is lifted up, He draws men to Himself. He compels them to come. The sheer force of His powerful love compels them to come.

But first the *real* Jesus must be lifted up!

4

The God-Man

I like to know where someone is coming from. If I am dealing with someone, I like to know where he has been, where he comes at me from.

With Jesus it is no different. As soon as I knew that He loved me, I wanted to know why. As soon as I believed that He was here, I wanted to know where He comes from, what He has been through, how He got here from there.

It is not good enough to glory in the great love of the magnificent Jesus. It is not good enough to know about the Jesus of today; we must know about the Jesus of history. No man can fully grasp the magnificence of Jesus merely by looking at the miracles which He performs today. We love Him more as we know more about where He comes from.

The Bible tells me where Jesus has been and what He has done. It tells the whole story in the Gospels of Matthew, Mark, Luke, and John. The story is so powerful that it comes tearing through the old, stodgy language of the King James Version. It is so strong, such a fantastic story, that it comes surging past the quaint vocabulary. It leaps off the pages of the Bible, straight into the heart of any man honest enough to listen.

Regardless of how many times I tell the story, hearing it again moves me to love Jesus more.

We call it Palm Sunday. Looking back on it, we know that it was the beginning of the end for Jesus here on this earth. It was a Jewish feast day in Jerusalem, and the streets were crowded and jammed with people from all over the countryside. They always poured into Jerusalem from the little towns on the holy feast days. Jesus was one of the people. He was no big shot from the big city. He was one of them, from the humble town of Nazareth. So on this holiday He came to Jerusalem, too, along with the twelve apostles.

A strange thing happened as Jesus came into the city that day. He had been preaching throughout the countryside for three years, healing the sick, raising the dead, holding the little children on His lap, and helping people in all kinds of trouble. He had preached a strong message of repentance and holy living and as His voice rang out over the Judean countryside, so did His reputation spread. People talked about Him. They told stories about Him over campfires late into the night. They repeated His words across breakfast and dinner tables in ten thousand homes. And they began to hope, to believe, to think that maybe He was for real, that maybe He *was* something special. They began to wonder if somehow, miraculously, a Messiah had indeed finally come to lead them.

And so as He rode into the city that day on a little donkey, the word spread through the bustling holiday crowds like fire through a dry hayfield. "Jesus is coming!" And spontaneously, without signal or warning, they rushed by the thousands to line the sides of the road to see Him pass. There was no plan, no organized effort —just a spontaneous burst of hope and joy and excitement that charged the crowd.

Somebody began to chant, *"Hosanna, hosanna."* A few more people took up the chant, and suddenly the massed crowds were singing it all together, singing out joyfully and strongly, with heads thrown back and voices ringing in a giant, swelling sound: *"Hosanna. Blessed is the King of Israel that cometh in the name of the Lord!"* (*See* Luke 19:38.)

It must have been a strange sight. Jesus, the son of a carpenter, a village boy from Nazareth, riding into town on the back of a donkey as the crowds stood by the thousands to see Him and cheer Him and call Him their king! He must have been a powerful, compelling person, even to those who didn't know who He was. Somehow He grabbed their attention and their respect, and once they had seen Him they never forgot His look, His voice, His sheer presence that dominated whatever setting He was in.

But the happy, holiday mood of that Palm Sunday soon was shattered by evil men who hated Jesus and had vowed to kill Him. The *hosanna*s stopped, and the streets grew quiet. And within a week the strong, gentle Jesus of Nazareth was a twisted, limp corpse. His body was battered and torn. His scalp was a mess of ugly, gaping gashes. His face was bruised and bloody. A hole as large as a man's fist was in His side. His back was puffy, raw, bits of flesh hanging from long, nasty cuts. And He was dead.

To the Pharisees, who hated Jesus for exposing their evil hearts to public view, just killing Jesus was not good enough. They weren't content to hire an assassin and have Him quietly murdered, knifed, or clubbed to death in a back alley. They could have killed Him that way, and it would have been much easier.

But they hated Him too much. They wanted not just to kill Him but to humiliate Him publicly, to disgrace Him before the crowds. They hated Him because He had called them snakes and scoundrels. He was the only man with the guts to stand in front of them and tell it like it really was. He called them snakes, hypocrites, whitewashed sepulchres, two-faced, lying thieves. And they hated Him with that black hatred of evil men who have been exposed for what they are.

So they plotted, they conspired, they attacked Him in the Garden of Gethsemane late one night and threw a whole team of paid liars against Him. They kicked Him and spit on Him. They cursed and slapped Him. And then the rough stuff started: the beatings, the flying fists as He stood defenseless with hands tied behind His back; His head and scalp ripped open with long, nail-like thorns.

No matter how often I think of the gentle, magnificent Jesus standing there, stripped and humiliated, being mugged by those drunken beasts, it makes my blood run hot and my anger rise and my heart beat faster, and I want to jump in there with Him and fight for Him and clean those dirty hoodlums out! Those cowards with their whips and chains and spears! Those bullies taking the gentlest man in all the world and kicking His face and spitting at that man who loved me so much! My instinct is to want to go after them, to scream for their blood, to drag them out from their holes and make them answer for their cruel, sadistic treatment of this man!

But Jesus would not allow that. He rebuked that attitude in Peter, and He would rebuke it in me. He could have blasted them on the spot. He could have wiped them all out with a single blow. He could have called all the angels of heaven to destroy His tormentors and rescue Him. He could have done it at any time.

But He refused to do so. He chose to suffer. Alone, He was alone, deserted by Peter and John and His fickle disciples, alone with the guards and their whips and fists. But He chose to suffer, and suffer He did. He bled, and grunted, and slumped to the floor. He moaned

and rolled His head from side to side as the nails split
His feet. He sweated and bled and doubled over in
pain. He collapsed and got back to His feet and grew
dizzy with the pain and the nausea and the hot sun.
But He never opened His mouth to condemn them. He
said nothing. He had courage as no man ever before or
since. He felt life slide away from Him, felt the horizon
spin and grow dim as He hung suspended, hanging by
those huge, ugly nails. And with His last breath He
loved those men, those brutal bullies who so tortured
Him.

What a magnificent man! What a matchless, over-
whelming display of guts and love!

When I heard that story for the first time, heard of
how Jesus Christ had been abused and killed, heard
how He had been framed and set up to die, it filled me
with awe. For the first time in my life I stood in awe of
a man so superior in every way to me, so much greater
in courage and strength. And when I learned that He
had done it all for me, gone through all that for me, it
was more than I could stand, more than I could believe!

Even now it chills me to think of it. I know that
Jesus thought of me when He hung on that cross on that
Golgotha hill. He thought of me when the fists smashed
His groin and the beard was jerked from His face. I
know that He suffered it for Nicky Cruz; He endured it
for Nicky Cruz. He did it all for me!

Oh, magnificent Jesus! How could You do it—how
could You do it for me, beautiful Jesus? I know where
You come from, Jesus, I know about that Sanhedrin

Court and the punishment and that long, sick climb up Calvary, Jesus! And now, to know that You are with me, that You stand here beside me in this room, is enough to make me fall on my knees and worship You today and every day! I know where You have been, Jesus, and what a big difference it makes to me to know that You loved me that much before I ever knew You!

5

He Is There!

If Jesus Christ is not alive, all Christians are fools.

If Jesus Christ is not alive this very minute, every minister in the world should be arrested for fraud.

If Jesus Christ is not alive and present right now in this room with you as you read this book, you should throw the book away without reading another word, because the entire book is a lie and you are wasting your time.

But Jesus is alive—literally, actually, genuinely alive —and He is present with you wherever you are—right now, as you read these words. Stop for a moment and look up from the page. Look at the four walls that surround you. Whether you are sitting in a bedroom, a library, an automobile, a living room, or a jail cell, look

45

at the place around you and *make* yourself realize that Jesus Christ of Nazareth is right now inside that room with you.

He is there!

As surely as *you* are there, *He* is there! It makes no difference whether you are a saint or a sinner, whether you pray five hours a day or have never prayed in your life, whether you feel that you know Jesus or not—He is still there, in that room with you, alive, real, just as if you could see Him, talk to Him, reach out and touch Him.

Can you imagine what an impact it would have if this strange, powerful man should materialize before your eyes and stand, in the flesh, in that place where you sit and read just now? It would numb your mind! It would shake you, stun you, fill you with awe and excitement. However impossible it seems, there is one thing in life you can be absolutely sure of: Jesus Christ is there with you now, and the fact that you cannot see Him does not make it any less true.

You say, "Oh, sure, God is everywhere. He is in the trees and flowers, the winds that blow and all of nature. God is everywhere, so He must be in this cup of coffee and in this room."

No! That is not what I am saying!

When I tell you that Jesus is there with you, I do not mean it in the sense that God is everywhere. I am not talking about some vague, shadowy presence that spreads over all the world. I am not talking about a spirit, an idea, an atmosphere of good that hovers over you. I am talking about a man—a real, living, flesh-and-blood man who had a beating heart and eyes that grew red and ached in the hot sun; a man with skin and bones and a back that hurt if He lifted something too heavy. I'm talking about a man with a voice that was strong and clear at times and soft and hoarse at other times—just like mine and yours. I'm talking about a man whose hands bulged with veins through which flowed real, warm, sticky blood and whose skin grew wet and slick with sweat when He walked too fast or worked too hard. I'm talking about a man who hollered when He stepped with bare feet on a sandspur, who laughed long and hard at the jokes of His friends, who grew quiet and pensive when He saw his mother getting old and turning gray.

When I tell you Jesus is there with you, don't think I am talking about a spirit, a ghost or spook, some mysterious something that hovers and swishes overhead like a holy-holy, hush-hush spirit. A *man* is there with you! I mean Jesus of Nazareth, who worked in a carpenter's shop and knew how it felt to jam a splinter up under His fingernail. That man Jesus is there with you!

"Why is He there?" you ask.

Good question. Why would He possibly be interested in that place where you are? That kitchen, that classroom, that front porch, that hotel room, that den where you sit with the kids' toys scattered over the floor and the carpet needing to be vacuumed—what would Jesus of Nazareth be doing in that place?

He is there because you are there!

That's right!

He knows you—by name, nickname, middle name— He knows you. And He loves you. He has been loving you since before you were old enough to say your first word. Since you toddled on fat little legs, those first baby steps, He has loved you and waited for you and watched you grow. He was there the first day you went off to school, and that day you locked yourself in the bathroom at home and cried, He was there, too. He followed you every step of the way, right through the hopscotch and all the running and chasing on the playground and when you first started to date, hardly knowing what to do with yourself, He was there with you then, too.

And now you are grown, and you need help to put your life together. You are threatened by all the evil of an evil world, and you are alone and vulnerable. Do you think this Jesus who has been with you so long would now grow distant and cold; would He now pull back and forget how He bled for you and how He has loved you?

No way!

He is there! He is there wherever you are because He has followed *you* there. Because He loves you! He has broken in and shown you who He is and made you aware of Himself. And now you are no longer a little child. Now you can know Him and talk to Him. You can embrace Him and pull Him close to your bosom right there where you are.

He came a long way to be there with you now. He came past a million sorrows and through the agonies of death to be with you now. When they pulled His body off that cross two thousand years ago, He seemed to be dead, as any other man dies. But He was not. While they were anointing His limp, pale body with spices, wrapping it in a burial cloth, and laying it in that cave tomb, Jesus was in the pit of hell, battling death and sin and defeating it once and for all. He was fighting Satan for power over you. And when He won the victory and stepped from that grave, it was almost as if He had stepped into a time machine and out again. Nothing could stop Him now! Nothing could bind Him now!

Death could not hold Him—He had faced it and whipped it. The grave could not bind Him—He had laid down in it and had come fighting up by the sheer power of who He was to shatter its grip on Him. Sin could not touch Him—He had looked in its face and spit in its eye and declared Himself its conqueror. Time could not control Him—He had shown that He was not subject to time, that He was instead its master. He had nothing to hold Him back now, nothing to prevent Him from coming to every man, wherever he is, and that is how He comes there to be present with you right now.

To Jesus, you are no different from the people whom He met on the roads of Judea, in the little towns, and by the seashore. He moved easily and naturally among them because He was one of them. He preached in the open air. He held the children in His lap. He touched the eyes of the blind with gentle hands and made them see again. And with the same hands He whipped the money changers from the Temple. He spoke with a soft, firm voice to the adulterous woman lying in the dirt before Him, forgiving and blessing her. And with the same voice He lashed the Pharisees and hypocrites until they were stung and angry and could only slink away. He walked among the people and He loved them, and His anger never fell on the sincere, the openhearted, the bruised sinner who sought to change. His anger was for the pompous and the proud who used the vocabulary of the church and the trust of the people for their own sinful gain.

Jesus never looked on a crippled man or a diseased child without concern and compassion. He never met a messed-up, confused person without reaching out to help. He never talked to a sinner who was tired of his sins without forgiving him and making him clean. He never met a man or a woman He didn't love.

Are we different from those people of Jesus' day?

Are we any less to Jesus than they were?

Are our cancers less fatal than theirs? Is our blindness less dark? Is our anxiety and sickness of heart less painful? Is our sin less terrible, our loneliness less real? When someone we love dies, is our grief less numbing and unbearable?

Of course not.

If you trade your suit for a robe, your automobile for a donkey, your language for that of the ancient East, if you strip yourself down to what is really you, you are no different from any man whom Jesus saw and touched and loved in Judea so long ago. And Jesus knows that. So He comes to you, there where you are, and He does for you all the things He did for them when He was on the earth as a carpenter's son.

He wants to forgive you of your sin. He wants to heal you of your sickness. He wants to keep you from anxiety and fear and guilt. He wants to free you from every kind of bondage. And He is there with you now to do it. He is a wonderful, magnificent Saviour!

THE
MAGNIFICENT
FATHER

6

Then and Now

The man's throat feels like sandpaper, it is so rough and scratchy and dry. But he has swallowed and swallowed and now he cannot swallow again, and the throat gets worse. He is dizzy and weak and he hurts in a hundred places.

But most of all he is scared. He has been scared before, but never like this. He is scared because he knows he is going to die. He is tied to a cross, and the cross is on a hill. By opening his eyes he can see the garbage dump at the base of the hill, and without opening them he can smell it. It stinks and he is sick and scared and about to die.

All his life he has been a thief. Since he can remember he has stolen, and now he is dying for it, tried and sentenced and dying as he always feared he would, crucified, just a matter of hours before the soldier breaks his legs—and he hopes he is dead by then because he thinks he cannot bear the pain if he is still alive.

He fights the sick waves of unconsciousness that wash over him. Now, he knows, is the time to do it. It will soon be too late. The Prophet Jesus is dying beside him, a few feet away on another cross. He has heard of this Jesus for two years now, and long ago saw a little boy whose arm He had straightened. And now he has watched Him here all day on this ugly, horrible hill, and somehow he has felt the strong vibrations from that Jesus, and he knows it must be true what they said of Him. He must somehow be different from all of us. He must somehow be different.

And the terrible, choking sadness of a lifetime rises in him and for a moment blocks out the pain and he gathers his strength and shouts in a croaking, whispering cry, "Jesus! Jesus, remember me when You come into Your kingdom!"

And the Prophet Jesus turns His head a half-turn in the thief's direction. The blood is caked on His face and streaked down His chest. "Today. You will be with Me in heaven today." The words come to him in a thin, pale voice, but the sound goes into his ears and through the head and down into his body and his heart and his soul that he thought was no longer there, and it fills him up with a strange, warming peace. The unconsciousness comes back now, stronger than ever, but he does not fight it this time. He lets it come. He embraces it. He leans against it and it takes him and he dies.

The Scriptures give this account:

39 And one of the malefactors which were hanged railed on him, saying, If thou be Christ, save thyself and us.

40 But the other answering rebuked him, saying, Dost not thou fear God, seeing thou art in the same condemnation?

41 And we indeed justly; for we receive the due reward of our deeds: but this man hath done nothing amiss.

42 And he said unto Jesus, Lord, remember me when thou comest into thy kingdom.

43 And Jesus said unto him, Verily I say unto thee, To day shalt thou be with me in paradise.

44 And it was about the sixth hour, and there was a darkness over all the earth until the ninth hour.

45 And the sun was darkened, and the veil of the temple was rent in the midst.

46 And when Jesus had cried with a loud voice, he said, Father, into thy hands I commend my spirit: and having said thus, he gave up the ghost.

* * *

She was a hooker—a prostitute—and she came forward in a large crowd of people who responded to my altar invitation during a crusade in Dallas, Texas. I never knew her name but I knew her story, and I was moved by the way that she had allowed Jesus to turn her life completely around and set her on a new course.

But her problems were not over when she came forward to be saved that night. She returned home cleansed of sin but not of the ravages of sin; and, only a few days after the crusade left Dallas, she got the news. Syphilis. She was infected with syphilis, and not all the tears in the world could cure her of this terrible, lingering reminder of her old way of life.

She was distraught when she got the news from her doctor. Knowing nothing to do but look to her newfound Saviour, she determined to lay her burden at the feet of Jesus. She placed a long-distance call from a pay phone booth, unwilling to call from home for fear of being overheard by her husband, with whom she was afraid to share her secret.

"Help me pray," she cried over the phone. "Please help ask Jesus to heal me!"

It may seem strange to some, but God has often blessed people to pray for someone whom they have never seen, never touched. And this was one of those times.

"Listen," I said. "Jesus is there with you and here with me in this office. Let's unite our hearts together in prayer."

And we prayed. I bowed my head in my office in North Carolina while she held the phone in Texas, and then I could hear her on the other end crying and giving thanks to God for her healing.

Her faith and the love of Jesus made her whole. I
met her later at a crusade in Little Rock, Arkansas. She
told me the end of her story: The syphilis was completely healed, there had been no communication of
the disease to her husband or baby, and her marriage
was strong and unshaken. She had the look of a woman
who knows the touch of a magnificent Jesus.

* * *

And another story of faith from God's Word:

But as he went, the crowds nearly suffocated
him. Among them was a woman, who had had a
chronic haemorrhage for twelve years and who had
derived no benefit from anybody's treatment. She
came up behind Jesus and touched the edge of his
cloak, and her haemorrhage stopped at once.

"Who was that who touched me?" said Jesus.
And when everybody denied it, Peter remonstrated,

"Master, the crowds are all round you and are
pressing you on all sides. . . ."

But Jesus said,

"Somebody touched me, for I felt that power
went out from me."

When the woman realised that she had not
escaped notice she came forward trembling, and
fell at his feet and admitted before everybody why
she had had to touch him, and how she had been
instantly cured.

"Daughter," said Jesus, "It is your faith that has healed you—go in peace."

Luke 8:42–48 PHILLIPS

*   *   *

The townspeople view her with contempt.

She is little more than a whore. She knows it; they know it; and she knows they know it. They cross the road and walk by on the other side when she passes. And when the men speak of her, on those long evenings when they gather to gossip outside their houses, they speak with a low, steady disgust and spit into the dusty ground as they say her name.

She has lived with five men, each for long enough to know them well, even for some long enough to love them, but she has been weak, too weak to stay home at night, too weak to say no to a handsome new face. All her life she has been that way—she doesn't understand why. She makes her vows and she means them and almost before the words are spoken she is breaking them again.

She hates herself. Deeply and truly she hates herself.

She knows that she is dirty and low and hopelessly soiled. And she hurts, because she is not too old to remember the good days, the days of innocence and virtue. She can recall the lighthearted promise of her girlhood, when her name was spoken in the town without contempt or filthy jesting. Most of all she hurts because she feels so dirty, so unclean, so cheap. She is old at thirty-one years, already old and used and dying inside.

She can no longer face the people of the town, the gentle old women, the teenagers who romp and play, the young housewives who come to draw water from the well. They come to stop and visit and chatter together at the well as much as to do the chore itself, and she cannot bear to hear their gossip and feel the gaze of their eyes. And most of all she cannot face the men, the men who have used her, touched and dirtied and discarded her, who have visited her in the dark of night and slinked away, better able to live with their sin than she is with hers.

So she goes alone to the well. She goes when others are eating, when families are sitting down to their meals, when the streets are almost empty. Leaving the home of a man, the latest of her many men, a man she needs more than she loves, she goes to draw water.

And there at the well it happens. There she meets a strange Nazarene, an out-of-towner. And he looks into her eyes without scorn, and talks to her. What He tells her is not idle talk. It is not the empty conversation of two people who have never met. He looks at her and tells her who she is and what she has done and how she feels inside. Gently, patiently, He shows her the most private parts of her heart. She sits stunned, transfixed, drawn to His words as to a magnet. And He heals her. From the inside out, He touches and heals her; magically, in a moment, He makes her clean again, chases away the memories that have haunted and shamed her, and breathes new, clean life into her.

She leaves the well without the water she came to draw, without the pot she came to draw it in, without the sin that brought her there in the middle of the day. And when she runs back through the streets, she runs with light, innocent feet, the feet of a young girl, and she laughs the happy, songlike laugh of a teenager. And she shouts the news to the people she meets, like a woman set free from a deep and cheerless prison.

7

I'm No Better Than God

I am a father.

If someone asked you, "Who is Nicky Cruz?" you might answer that he is a former gang leader, a Puerto Rican preacher, an ex-Mau-Mau warlord, a youth evangelist, or whatever. And all that is true.

But I am also a father. I have four daughters: Alicia, Laura, Nicole, and Elena Mia, ages thirteen, nine, seven, and three. So you must admit that I am a father, even though you might think of me as being something else altogether.

You may be able to steal my money, burn my house, slander my name, wreck my car, or tear holes in my lawn, and get away with it. But if you step on my kids, you're going to make me mad because, like most men, being a good father is very important to me.

I may lose money on an investment, have a year or two with low income, cut back on my wardrobe expenses, cancel my membership at the health club, and get very stingy when the man comes to collect for the United Fund. But you can bet your bottom dollar that when my kids sit down to the table to eat, there will be food in front of them three times a day—because nothing will keep me from being a good father.

Sometimes I get hard and callous just like the next guy. I may get cold and hardhearted and lose my sensitivity to the poor people in the ghetto or the starving millions in Biafra, or the feelings of my secretary when everything is going wrong for her at the office. But let one of my little girls crawl into my lap at the end of the day and I can't hold back the flood of loving, tender emotions inside—because nothing will keep me from being a good father.

Occasionally I may be too easy on myself, become soft in my self-discipline, and certainly I will let my neighbors get away with all types of bad behavior on our block. I may even overlook the gradual development of bad habits in a friend and never take the time to do or say anything about it to him. But if one of my girls starts down the primrose path toward a destructive habit, I come down hard and heavy on it at the earliest possible moment—because nothing will keep me from being a good father.

Am I better than God?

Of course not!

That's such a preposterous question that it sounds blasphemous just to ask it. No one with good sense would suggest for a moment that he is superior to God in any way. Yet there are many Christians who take pride in their own parenthood, and at the same time act as if God does not take seriously His role as a father.

God is a Father. You are His child. Every evidence of Scripture indicates that God takes his fatherhood just as seriously as you and I do. He is just as concerned with His children as we are with ours.

We do not call God our Father because some preacher dreamed it up. His role as a Father does not come from the imagination of a clever Christian writer who struck upon it to illustrate a point he wished to make. It did not begin in the writing of ancient church history. It comes from God Himself. It is God Himself who says that He is our Father, and in the Bible He reminds us of it over and over, in both the Old and New Testaments.

The fatherhood of God is not simply a figure of speech. It is a role of God, a part of God, one of the three faces of God by which He interacts with human beings.

Too many people try to make God whatever they want Him to be. They say, "God is this" and "God is that" without ever paying attention to what God Himself says He is. We cannot dream up clever ways to describe God and then expect Him to fit them. We cannot decide how to relate to God comfortably and conveniently, and then expect God to squeeze Himself into that relationship just to suit us. It is our job to learn from the Bible what God is and how He wants to relate to us, and then to fit ourselves into that role.

How do I know that God wants me to think of Him as a Father? The Bible tells me so! We see it clearly in the Lord's Prayer. Jesus Christ was telling His disciples how to pray, how to approach God, how to view Him and relate to Him: "And he said unto them, When ye pray, say, Our Father which art in heaven . . ." (Luke 11:2).

There it is! Jesus was asked by His disciples to teach them how to pray, and He was not engaging in idle phrase-making. He was telling them how to put their minds right to talk to God, how to get their heads straight when they wanted to communicate with the Almighty. "Look," He seems to say, "don't think about how small and unworthy you are, about how sinful you are and how righteous God is. Don't think about Him as a Judge or a Creator or a Mysterious Presence. Think of Him as your Father. You are His child. He is your Father. Call Him that. Think of Him as that. Start your conversations with Him by reminding yourself that He is your Father."

That reference to the fatherhood of God is, of course, only one of dozens. God promises the people of His church that this special relationship is available for everyone: ". . . I will receive you, And will be a Father unto you, and ye shall be my sons and daughters, saith the Lord Almighty" (2 Corinthians 6:17, 18). What a fantastic promise!

"Okay," you say, "I know that God is my Father. He is the Father of us all. He made us and we are all His creatures." True. But that concept of the fatherhood of God is out-of-date. Its time has passed. It is from the Old Testament and it is not good enough for today. All creatures of God—and that means all people everywhere—are His children in that sense of the word. In Old Testament days, God was Father simply because He was Creator. But that kind of fatherhood was universal and impersonal.

No more! God is my Father in a different way now. He is not my Father just in that Old Testament sense of the word but also in a new, personal, special kind of fatherhood that is reserved for born-again Christians only. He is my Father not just because He created me but now also because He adopted me as His child! I am His creature, but more than that I am His adopted son!

Listen to the Apostle Paul describe it:

For as many as are led by the Spirit of God, they are the sons of God. For ye have not received the spirit of bondage again to fear; but ye have received the Spirit of adoption, whereby we cry, Abba, *Father.* The Spirit itself beareth witness with our spirit, *that we are the children of God.*

Romans 8:14–16, author's italics

I was alone. I was homeless. I had no father to love me, protect me, provide for me. I was weak and vulnerable, like a little, runny-nosed boy standing in the cold with ragged clothes and an empty stomach. God was my Father—but only in the terribly meaningless sense that somewhere, long ago, He created me. That kind of fatherhood sounds impressive in the theology books but it was pretty empty stuff for someone pitifully in need of a personal, loving Father. I needed a sure-enough, honest-to-goodness, heavenly Father—a Father who could be with me here and now—a Father to pray to, to talk with, to depend on.

So God adopted me and made me His own personal child! It was just me and Him this time. None of that God-of-Creation kind of fatherhood, but a close, personal fatherhood. He chose *me* and embraced *me* and made *me* His son. What a totally magnificent Father!

God is my Father, so He *disciplines* me. I am not perfect, so I stray. Like a headstrong kid I try to do what I want instead of what God wants. I try to convince myself that what I am doing is right, but deep in my belly I have this hard knot that tells me that I am doing wrong. But I keep on anyway because I am flesh and flesh is sinful.

So God cracks me over the head. God, my Father, my loving Father, cracks me over the head until He gets my attention. He makes me look at myself and at Him. He makes me see how dirty I am and how clean

He is. He shakes me until all the silly ideas come loose and fall out of my head. He spanks me good! And then He picks me up, wipes my tears, and gives me a fresh, new start.

He is my Father, and He punishes me when I get out of line because that is what loving fathers do to disobedient sons.

God is my Father, so He *protects* me.
Even animals protect their offspring.
God my Father surely would do no less for me!

America has probably never been more dangerous for more people than it is right now. At least not since the early frontier days have the chances been greater than now that a person will not live to see the sunset when he heads out his front door every day. The rate of violent crime is high and going higher every day. More than fifty thousand people die each year in highway accidents. International travel has been made hazardous by a whole list of armed terrorist and guerilla groups in Ireland, the Middle East, Portugal, Africa, and Latin America.

It is no wonder that so many people live with so much anxiety every time they ride a subway, drive on the turnpike, or walk the streets at night.

I have an edge that lots of people don't have. I am a son of God. He is powerful. He knows everything. He can do anything. And, since He is my Father, He protects me in a special way. He has a plan for my life, and He is not willing to let me die before that plan is worked out. He looks after me, just as I look after my daughters. They are sometimes afraid, too—afraid of big dogs, afraid of the dark, afraid of all those things that hold danger for sweet little girls.

But when I am with them—well, that is different! I am their father, and as a good father I will keep the danger away. They know that, and with me they are not afraid.

Would my Father do less for me?

God is my Father, so He *provides* for me. What good father does not provide for his children? Suppose I come home one afternoon and meet my daughter going out the door: "Where are you going?" I ask.

"I'm hungry, so I'm going out to see if I can find some food to eat somewhere," she says.

"But how are you going to find any food? You are just a little girl. Don't you know that if you'll just wait awhile I'll have food for you to eat?"

"But how can I be sure?" she complains. "After all, you may feed me and you may not. And I am getting a bit hungry already and there is no food on the table yet," she argues.

"Ridiculous!" you say. And it *is* ridiculous. But that is exactly how we treat God. He is our Father and He tells us that He will provide for our needs, but we get a bit behind with our payments, or the budget gets the least bit stretched, and Boom! We panic! Suddenly we quit trusting God and begin to worry about where the money is coming from. We start trying to figure out

ways to make it on our own. We wonder if God knew
what He was doing when He started the whole thing.

God provides. That is a rule of life. It is as de-
pendable as snow in the winter and grass in the spring.
It is as sure as the ground under our feet and the sky
over our heads. God is our Father and He provides for
our needs.

I don't know everything there is to know about
theology. I am not a Greek scholar. I am just a Puerto
Rican street kid whom God picked up from the slums
in New York and made into a disciple and a minister.
So I don't know all the ins and outs of higher criticism
and religious philosophy and all that. But there is one
thing I know. I have known it since the old days in
Brooklyn when Jesus first found me. I know that God is
my Father. And I am glad to be His little child.

Maybe that is where God wants me to start. Maybe
that is the most important thing of all.

8

The Silence

Some people are afraid of God—really, terribly afraid of God. They are so afraid of God that they never enjoy living for Him. They never feel good about themselves, never relax, never just sit back and enjoy themselves. They serve God because they are scared of going to hell, or because they believe something bad will happen to them if they don't worship Him.

What a shame!

What a total waste!

What an awful way to live—always uptight and scared to death that God is going to zap them if they do something wrong! I don't believe God wants us to be afraid of Him. I believe He wants us to be comfortable with Him, to relax and enjoy His presence, to feel good when we are with Him.

We talk about God-fearing men when we mean God-respecting men. We speak of "fearing" God to say that a person is aware of Him and respects Him. That is, of course, not what I am objecting to. I am speaking of men who are actually afraid of God in the way that children are afraid of big, strange dogs.

And it is no wonder. We hear so much about the power of God to punish evil, destroy sin, and squash Satan—it is no wonder people are afraid of Him. The truth is that God *does* punish. He *does* bring us into line when we stray. He *does* spank us when we, like little children, neglect to do what we know is right. But God is a good Father, not a mean one. He punishes us in love, not in anger. His punishment is always exactly what we need—not too light to be ignored, and not too severe to cripple us. The Bible says that God "chasteneth" those whom He loves (*see* Hebrews 12:6). Doesn't that sound just like a father?

Picture this scene: A man comes home from work and finds his son sitting on the floor, marking on the wall with a crayon. He jerks the child to his feet, takes him into the kitchen, pulls a butcher knife from a drawer, and cuts off the kid's hand. That's punishment, brother, but it is also stupid. It is insanity! And it is ridiculous to expect God to act that way. He doesn't jerk up His children at the slightest offense and wipe them out! God the Father disciplines His children.

There can be no doubt about that. But He disciplines
gently. He disciplines in love.

God has whipped me good a few times. There have
been times when I wanted to go my own way. Like a
little child, I felt overprotected by my heavenly Father.
I wanted to do my own thing, and I wasn't patient
enough to wait for God to work things out for me. Once
I went into the retail clothing business. I didn't pray
about it or seek God's guidance. I just did it, whether
God liked it or not, because I like fine clothes and I
wanted to make some money. That was wrong—I knew
it then but I went ahead anyway. There was nothing
wrong with owning a clothing store, obviously, but it
was wrong to go into any venture without praying about
it and getting God's approval first.

There have been other times when I have done
wrong, times that have hurt my heavenly Father. When
I was in Bible school, I became so frustrated with my
lack of progress as a student and a young preacher that I
decided to forget the whole thing and go back home to
New York. I was lonely and homesick in California,
and I wondered if it was worth it, so I made up my mind
to quit—quit school, quit the ministry, quit the struggle
to learn more about the Lord and the Scriptures. That
was wrong. It was a betrayal of all that God had done
for me. It was wrong, and I knew it, but I was going to
do it anyway.

There have been other times when I have sinned,
when I have done wrong. And every time it has hurt my
Father, and He has disciplined me for it.

When I first became a Christian, I thought if I did wrong, I would be killed in a plane crash, or a car would run into me, or I would have an accident of some sort. But that is not the way the Father disciplines His wayward children. Instead, He sends what I call the "Silence."

When I do wrong, God takes His peace away from me. He reaches down into my heart and takes away the joy that He put there when I became His child. He stops His voice in my life. I can no longer hear Him. Where His voice was there is only Silence, and that is a terrible, terrible feeling. It gives me a great restlessness. It tears me apart. I look at Jesus and I know that I have done an ugly thing to Him, that I have hurt Him.

It is similar to hurting one's wife. If a man loves his wife and he does wrong to her, it hurts him. He feels miserable. That is **how** it is with sinning against the Father. I feel miserable. So I come back to the right path, not because I'm afraid of being zapped, but because of the love that God has taken away. The joy is gone. I want to feel that closeness again. My chest feels as if it will crush with the weight of that terrible Silence of God. I have that hurting pain inside because I know I have hurt my Father.

Have you ever had a time when God put that Silence in your life? When you almost think that He is not there at all, that He has gone someplace else? When you try to pray and you feel that nobody is listening?

I think to myself, *Nicky, you are a smart man,* and I try to work my way out of that Silence. I begin to call on every resource, to pull every string. I pull the theology string, the philosophy string, the psychology string. Then sometimes I try to do it by sheer force, to pray and shout and storm my way out of the Silence. I pray loud and hard, "Hallelujah, hallelujah," and all that. And nothing happens. I say, "Maybe I need to fast," and I fast, but it does no good. The Silence is still there.

And finally I am forced to look squarely at myself and see me as God sees me. I have to admit that I have been carnal and bad. With a heart that is bursting with sorrow, I confess my wrongdoing and I throw my arms around my Father's neck. I tell Him how I feel, and I rest in His arms, and the peace and joy come flooding back.

My Father has disciplined me, and it has brought me back to Him! He hasn't wiped me out, destroyed me, come down so hard on me that I am never able to get on my feet again. He hasn't beaten me over the head until I finally change my ways. He simply takes away His peace. And His presence has been so good to me, His love so sweet, that I am drawn back to His arms, like a child who climbs, teary-eyed, into his daddy's lap after a spanking.

I am so glad that my Father loves me enough to punish me. It may sound fine for a father to say that he will let his children do whatever they want, so that the children can make decisions on their own—hoping they will come back to the straight-and-narrow of their own accord. But that can be a cop-out. Sometimes they don't come back. Sometimes they can't come back because they are dead, or their minds are blown by drugs, or somehow it is too late. I'm glad God doesn't let me stray too far before He busts me good and brings me back before it is too late. He stops me before I have a chance to mess myself up permanently.

Have you ever seen a parent who lets his children say rude, sassy things because he thinks they are cute? That's like feeding a little monkey. He is so cute and funny, and you feed him all the bananas he wants. But one day you turn around and that cute little monkey has become a gorilla. He now is out of control. You should have controlled him when you could, but you didn't and now he comes back to haunt you. Our sins are that way. They grow little by little, until finally they separate us from God. They eat us alive. They kill us.

It is the discipline of a magnificent Father that keeps that from happening.

David is one of my favorite Bible characters because he knew what it was to stray from God, to be disciplined, and to return to his Father. He knew the Silence of God. He knew what it was to lose the peace of God. He sinned. He saw a beautiful woman take her clothes off, and he was willing to kill her husband to make love to her. That hurt God because David had been a special, favorite son.

But God did not let David wander away so easily. He knew that David would be lost if he didn't repent. No matter that he was a great king and all that. He still would have been lost. So God disciplined him. He sent a prophet to push David back toward what he knew was right. David had enough sense to listen to the prophet, and to the Silence of God, and make his way back to his heavenly Father.

Other men have known the Silence. How do you suppose Jonah felt, leaning over the rail of that old ship as it pushed off from the dock and headed out to sea? He had known God and loved God and now he had deserted God and he was running. What do you suppose he felt as the wind began to blow, the water became choppy and rough, and the storm began to develop? I think I know what Jonah felt. I think he felt the Silence of God. Where once a peace and serenity had been, now there was a great, frightening Silence. More fearsome than the storm or the anger of the crewmen or the great fish was that terrible Silence inside his soul.

Samson must have known the Silence. He was specially touched by God. He was a superstar even before he became a full-grown man, with strength like no man ever had before him, with a reputation that made him a hero wherever he went. But Samson got out of line, and God withdrew from him. When God departed from Samson, so did the power and the special grace. So Samson stood in a Philistine dungeon, eyes not seeing, hair sheared from his head, and he felt the great, crushing Silence. Where the voice of God had been, there was nothing but Silence. And Samson came back.

There was never a man who relished the presence
of God more than Simon Peter did. Peter was a man of
action and noise. He laughed loudly. He did things
colorfully. He moved on a big scale, with moments of
towering anger and childlike delight. He loved God
deeply and emotionally, without holding anything back.
He knew the closeness of God's presence; he knew the
warmth of God's embrace.

But Peter was human. He was scared that night in
the Garden of Gethsemane, and at the sight of Jesus
being dragged away by Roman soldiers, there came a
sharply multiplying fear for his own safety, a desperation
to save his own hide. So Peter did the cowardly thing.
He turned chicken. He stood outside the Sanhedrin
Court through that dark, sick night, and three times he
denied Jesus. Three times he turned his back on God,
each time with more cursing and more blaspheming
than before. It was a time for courage, but Peter was
scared, and he turned his back on the God he knew and
loved.

Then the rooster crowed. And the Silence came. It
came suddenly to Peter, like a flash flood. It filled him
up, an aching, hurting Silence so real it was almost
physical—a pain, a longing for God that was suddenly
greater than the fear. And the Silence in the courtyard
of the Sanhedrin that night drove Peter back to God.
He never left after that. He clung to his Father. He
never strayed again. He was beaten and jailed, arrested
and attacked, threatened and tortured and finally killed,
but he never strayed again.

Jesus Christ Himself felt the Silence of God the Father, not because He had sinned, not because He had strayed, but because He took my sins and your sins onto Himself. That is literally what Jesus Christ did at Calvary. He took all the sins of Nicky Cruz and of every other person in the world, and accepted the guilt and the punishment for them. That punishment included the crown of thorns, the beatings and the ridicule, the nails and the crucifixion and the death which He suffered. And that punishment also included the Silence of God.

"My God, my God, why hast thou forsaken me?" (Matthew 27:46). Those are the most heart-wrenching words in Scripture. They are the most tragic, the most filled with pain. Jesus, that man of peace and goodness, hangs on the cross, face white and bruised, blood dripping from His body to the ground below, and through His agony He feels the Silence as God the Father turns His face from Him. "My God, why hast thou forsaken me?" Jesus embraced my sins; God turned away from Him; and Jesus, who had quietly endured all the suffering of that Black Friday, cried out in pain as He felt the Silence of God.

Keep me tender, Father. Keep me hungry for Your love. And when I do wrong, whip me, Father, until I crawl up into Your lap and hug You close and feel that I am Your child again.

9

Protected by
the Father

Last year I finished a crusade in Johannesburg, South
Africa, and boarded a South African Airways jumbo jet
bound for home. We were scheduled to stop in Luanda,
Angola, to refuel en route to London, where I would
change planes for New York and home.

It was about 10:30 P.M. and dark as we made our
approach into the Luanda airport. There were 287
passengers aboard. As we neared the ground, I heard the
sound of guns firing sharply from the ground beneath
us. Then with a jolt, a lurch, and many bumps, we
landed on the runway. The 747 jetliner was immediately
surrounded by jeeps and dozens of highly excited Por-
tuguese soldiers. We sat on the ground for two hours as
the plane's tires were changed, the fuselage and under-

carriage examined, damage from bullet holes checked out; and finally we were allowed to take off again.

We headed back to Johannesburg, our London destination temporarily forgotten. No way we were going to London in a plane full of bullet holes! We flew all night at five thousand feet. The crying started with the women, spread to the children, and continued all night. Oxygen masks kept popping out of their ceiling panels, and there was a general state of panic and hysteria until we arrived at Johannesburg at 7:00 A.M.

We later learned that we had been fired on by a band of African revolutionaries who had somehow staked out a spot near the Luanda airport and were trying to shoot us from the sky.

A reporter interviewed me about the incident after I was safely back in the United States. He wanted to know if I had been scared, and I told him not at all. I was being completely honest. Never for a moment did I worry about that flight because my heavenly Father had told me long before that I would not die in an airplane crash. "Look," I told the reporter, "those people shouldn't have worried. With me on the plane, there's no way it could have gone down, because God has promised me that!"

That may sound strange to you, but I believe in a God who is a Father to me. And I believe that He will protect me. I fly so much that, a few years ago, I started to get the shakes about planes. So I prayed about it. It was getting to be a real problem. God answered my prayer by assuring me that I would not die in a plane

crash. I believe Him. He is my Father and I trust Him.
So I don't worry about flying anymore.

I may die of snakebite, be killed in a car wreck, be
kicked to death by a mule, or die of pneumonia at the
age of 103. I don't know about any of that. But one
thing I know: I will not die in a plane crash. God told
me so and, however simplistic it sounds, that's just how
much I trust Him.

A good father protects his children. When there are
so many things that can go wrong, so much danger
around, God treats me like a little child of His. He
watches over me. I believe that Christians emphasize
the evil that can be done to them by Satan, and virtually
ignore the protection of God the Father that is a constant part of our lives. We talk about demons constantly
and ignore angels. I believe that angels are just as real as
demons are. If we Christians could use our spiritual eyes
to see the forces that constantly work to keep us safe, we
might have a whole new respect for God the Father.

It would be foolish, of course, for me to be so reliant
upon God's protection that I fail to do whatever I can to
take care of myself. God's protection doesn't give me a
license to break the laws of nature and expect to get
away with it. If I jump off a cliff, I probably will get
smashed on the ground below—no matter how good my
Christian experience may be! If I eat too much, I'll get
sick and fat. If I smoke habitually, I'll probably get lung
cancer. If I go to sleep at the wheel of my car, I might
wake up in heaven!

The point is that being God's son does not automatically relieve me of the responsibility to use my head. Spirituality doesn't always overcome stupidity. If I behave stupidly, God doesn't guarantee that He will always be there to bail me out.

And being God's child does not mean that nothing bad will ever come my way. Many good Christians meet death by accidents or violence. When that happens, we can only believe that God knows what He is doing, that He has a higher purpose, a better plan, for that person. Things can happen in life that are worse than death, and God might take a Christian home to protect him from some terrible thing that lurks in the future.

But those times are rare. I am convinced that God *does* place His hand personally on His children and protect them. I am convinced that there is a safety, a real physical safety, in being a child of God. I believe that God knows me by name, that He cares about me personally, that He broke into my life dramatically to save me from sin, and that He continues to intervene to give me a special supernatural protection from danger. And He does the same for you if you are His child.

Look at it this way: When you become a Christian, the devil begins to gun for you, and it takes the special hand of God just to keep things even! The closer a man gets to God, the more Satan hates him, and the harder he tries to destroy him. Satan is powerful, more powerful than any human being. And he can use that power to threaten your life. He comes after you to kill you!

Do you think God, your Father, will stand for that?

No way! He sees what Satan is trying to do and wraps you in an invisible shield that protects you from him.

I had a neighbor once who didn't like me. He would like to have smacked me in the nose; at the very least, he would have enjoyed cussing me out a few times. But he never did, because he was afraid of me. So what did he do? He picked on my kids! Since he was angry with me and was afraid to take me on personally, he tried to hurt me by treating my children badly.

Satan is just that kind of coward! He hates God but is afraid to tackle Him head-on. The devil has been clobbered by God so many times that he doesn't have the guts to fight Him anymore. So he picks on God's children instead. He tries to injure and hurt us, simply because he is mad at God and we are God's children.

But God won't let it happen! He protects us, day and night, in all kinds of danger, when we are conscious of His presence and when we are not. Like a loving father watching over a sleeping child, God our magnificent Father protects you and me!

I learned about God's protection at an early point in my life as a Christian. Only a few weeks after I went forward at the Saint Nicholas Arena to surrender my life to Jesus, I found myself in danger from gang members who were determined not to let me walk away from my old life without a fight. I had a reputation on the streets in those days in New York, and it wasn't a good one. I was known as a mean, bloodthirsty fighter, and there were plenty of enemies out there in the streets who wanted a piece of me. In the old days I would have been ready to go at them with a knife or a gun or whatever I could get my hands on. I had been fiercely proud of my ability to stay alive in the toughest, most violent area of the Brooklyn slums.

But now it was different. I had surrendered my gun to the police, thrown away my knife, and for the first time in years I was on the streets with no weapon of any kind. I felt naked. But it was a good feeling because even then I knew that I was God's little boy, and He would look after me.

A few weeks after my conversion, I went to a little Spanish church called Iglesia de Dios Juan 3:16 to give my testimony. It was the first church service I had ever attended inside a real church building, and one of the first times I testified about my conversion experience. It felt great, and I walked from the little church building with a strong sense of God's presence.

What happened then shook me rudely to my senses. The people were still milling around the vestibule and standing out front on the sidewalk. I was still shaking hands when I walked out the front door. Just then two cars across the street roared to life. I heard a woman scream. Glancing in that direction I saw gun barrels sticking out the windows and recognized some of the Bishops, bitter enemies of my old Mau Mau gang. They began shooting wildly in my direction as the cars jerked away from the curb. People were falling down in front of the church and running wildly back into the building trying to escape the flurry of bullets. I ducked behind a door as bullets smacked into the stone beside me. The cars sped off into the night.

God was with me. No doubt about it. He was watching over me. That same night He proved it to me again.

I was walking home from the church and paused along the street to talk with a friend named Loca, a girl from my old gang. As we chatted under a streetlight, I felt viselike hands grab me from behind. I wrenched my head around to see Joe, a member of the Bishops.

I was struggling to get loose when I saw the knife in his right hand. He held me from behind with his left hand around my neck while he swung the blade over my shoulder toward my heart. I threw my right hand up to ward off the eight-inch blade and it stabbed me in the hand between my ring finger and little finger, going all the way through my hand and barely grazing my chest.

I spun around and he slashed at me again. "I'm gonna kill you this time," he hissed. "You think you can get away from me by hiding behind a church, then baby, you're wrong. I'm gonna do the world a favor and kill a chicken who's turned square."

He moved toward me and jabbed the knife at my stomach. I jumped back and snatched a radio aerial off a parked car. Now the odds were even. In my hand, the aerial was as deadly as his switchblade.

I circled him, slashing the air with the metal rod. I was back in my own element now. I felt confident

I could kill him. I thought ahead, knowing from experience what his next move would be. When he lunged at me with his knife, I would dance back and catch him off balance. I could blind him with a backhanded swing and paralyze or kill him with the second blow.

I held the antenna in my left hand; my right hand, dripping with blood, I held in front of me to ward off his knife.

"C'mon, baby," I whispered. "Try it once more. Just once more. It'll be your last."

The boy's eyes were narrowed with hate. I knew I'd have to kill him because nothing else would stop him.

He started toward me and I stepped back as the knife whizzed by my stomach. Now! He was off balance. I brought the antenna back to whip it across his unprotected face.

Suddenly, it felt as though the hand of God grabbed my arm. *Turn the other cheek.* The voice was so real it was audible. I looked on this Bishop not as the enemy but as a person. I felt sorry for him, standing there in the night spitting curse words with hate written on his face. I could picture myself just a few weeks before, standing in the dark street trying to kill an enemy.

I prayed. For the first time, I prayed for myself. "God, help me."

The Bishop regained his balance and looked up at me. "What you say?"

I said it again. "God, help me." He stopped and stared at me.

All this time Loca had stood frozen in her tracks, watching the fight. Suddenly she sprang into action and ran to my side, thrusting the neck of a broken whiskey bottle into my hand. "Slit him open, Nicky."

The boy started to run. "Throw it at him, Nicky, throw it!"

I pulled back my arm but instead of throwing the bottle at the fleeing Bishop, I threw it against the side of the building.

Then I took my handkerchief and wrapped it around my badly bleeding hand. The blood soaked through and Loca ran up the steps to her room and brought me a bath towel to absorb the blood. She got me to the emergency room of a nearby hospital where surgeons operated on my hand, and to this day it is as good as ever.

I believe God kept me alive that night. I don't blame Joe, or whoever fired those shots at me on the church steps. I blame Satan. I believe he was out to get me, to push me to the edge of death, watch me squirm and break, then shove me on over the brink. But God would not allow it. He protected me from the dangers of that unfair fight.

You and me against Satan—now there's a mismatch for you! We can never fight him evenly on our own. But when our heavenly Father comes to the rescue, the odds turn dramatically in our favor. Satan is like the bully on the block who suddenly is confronted by the father of the little kid whom he has been shoving around. He pouts and shouts for a moment, and then he runs!

Give the devil credit—at least he has enough sense to know when he is outmuscled. He never threatens me the way he once did—not since I made it clear to him who my Father is!

10

A Nickel-and-Dime God?

Most people ask a question when they want to know something.

Not Jesus.

When Jesus asked a question, He didn't want information. He already knew everything. When He asked a question it was because He wanted to make a strong and powerful point. His questions were like dynamite.

Listen to this question that Jesus asked His disciples one day:

Or what man is there of you, whom if his son ask bread, will he give him a stone? Or if he ask a fish, will he give him a serpent? If ye then, being evil, know how to give good gifts unto your children,

how much more shall your Father which is in
heaven give good things to them that ask him?
Matthew 7:9–11

Jesus may have used a question, but He was not
asking His disciples for information. He was *telling*
them something, and what He was saying is strong stuff.
"You people think you are good fathers because you
give good things to your children," He was saying, "and
yet you are always afraid God is not going to take care of
you. What kind of Father do you think He is? Don't
you realize that He is a better Father for His spiritual
children than you are for your earthly children? He will
provide for you! He will give you everything you need!
Just relax and believe that He will!"

And so He will. It is as sure as night follows day:
your Father will provide for you.

It is amazing how many Christians do not really
believe that simple fact. They say they believe it, but
they do not. They worry all the time. They pile up
money and investments and insurance policies and all
kinds of security. They act as if the weight of the whole
world is on their shoulders, and all the time they have a
heavenly Father who is standing there, willing to share
the burden.

Jesus felt sorry for people like that. He pointed out
to them the flowers growing in the open field. "Look at
those flowers," He said. "Flowers don't know anything.
They aren't smart. They don't work hard. They aren't
very industrious. But they don't have anything to worry

about because when the spring comes I give them a new set of clothes. Just like that. I just lay it on them—and they are more beautiful than the robes of a king!" Jesus used that illustration to show how foolish it is to become anxious and worried about where the provisions of life are coming from. "Relax," He was saying. "Just let Me take care of everything." (*See* Matthew 6:28–34.)

Early in my ministry I worried a lot about paying the bills and maintaining an income that would support my family. I would become anxious if things looked bad temporarily. But finally I prayed through all that. I decided to put it in the hands of my heavenly Father. "You worry about it, God," I said. "I don't know what I'm doing. I'm just working hard for You and doing what I think is right, God. So I'm not going to worry about it anymore. You take care of it, okay, Lord?"

And it was almost as if God my Father leaned way out over the balcony of heaven and shouted at me, *Nothing to worry about, son! I've got everything under control!*

The money started coming in. People began to give to my ministry as never before. The dream I had of opening centers to care for wayward young people came true as a result of the rich way that my Father provided.

Now, whenever I start to get uptight about material things, I can hear the Father say, *Nothing to worry about!* So I don't worry. Of course I have life insurance. Of course I keep a small savings account. Of course I try to use my personal income wisely. But I am not interested in piling up huge amounts of money, and I don't believe any Christian should feel that he needs to do so in order to be secure. There is no security there. Banks can close. Jewels can be stolen. Stocks and bonds can lose their value.

But not my Father! He is my true security! He wants me to love Him and honor Him and leave the security problems to Him. He is not pleased with Nicky Cruz spending all his time and energy and attention trying to accumulate money.

You spend your time doing My work, the Father says, *and let Me take care of the nickel-and-dime stuff!*

"But God," I say, "what about my retirement?"

Just do My work, son. Everything's going to be all right.

"But what about the money for my kids' education?"

Just do My work, son. Everything's going to be all right.

"But what if I run out of money?"

Just do My work, son. I'll take care of the rest.

And then I look at my four daughters, my four precious daughters. I look at my Alicia, my firstborn, tall and serious and starting to grow into a woman. I look at my Laura, with that dark, pretty face and the soft, smooth skin of her mother. I look at little Nicole, my first-grader, still seeing the world with those big, innocent brown eyes. I look at Elena Mia, my baby, with that short, curly hair, always waving her chubby arms and making happy baby sounds.

And when I see those four sweet girls, and I know

that they are bone of my bone and flesh of my flesh, and I hear them call me "Daddy," I know that I would go anywhere, do anything, bear any burden, to love them and care for them and provide for their needs. Before I would hear them cry from hunger, I would be hungry myself. Before I would see them cold and shivering, I would strip the clothes from my back to give them. Before I would see them starving and in need, I would give everything I have. I would die for them.

And then the question comes from Jesus: "If ye then, being evil, know how to give good gifts unto your children, how much more shall your Father which is in heaven give good things to them that ask him?" (Matthew 7:11).

When Jesus asks a question, it hits like a hammer! Of course He will provide! He could no more leave me alone and destitute than I could leave my own children outside in the dark on a cold, rainy night! He is my Father, and it is important for me to remember that, to keep it in focus, to understand all that it can mean.

When we talk about the provision of God, most people automatically think of material things. God does provide financially. He has done so many times in my life and ministry. The history of the Christian church has been one of God the Father miraculously providing the financial needs of His children. It started in Bible times. Even in the Old Testament, the Father put food on the table before He would let His little children starve. Sometimes He dropped the food from the sky. Sometimes He sent it in a raven's mouth. Sometimes He let it grow up out of the ground naturally. But He never let His children starve.

Why should God change now?

Why should He become stingy after all this time?

Why should He treat us in the 1970s like little beggar kids, when throughout history He has always given His children the best?

God provides in many ways. Money is not the only thing He gives to His children. There are other things we need, sometimes even more urgently than we need material goods.

The Father provides people. You can have money piled up to your ears and be the most miserable man in town if you are lonely. Human beings need other human beings, and God knows that. Obviously, He can take care of that need, too.

Why not? He is God, after all! He made every one of us. He knows the number of hairs on our heads. He knows when we sit down and when we get up again. He calls us by name. And He is not so preoccupied with money that He would carefully supply our financial needs and still leave us lonely and miserable for want of other people in our lives.

God gave me Gloria. He knew I needed her. He knew she needed me. God my Father was there when we met the first time, when she got angry with me for being rude to her, and when I finally asked her for the first date. He was there when I asked her to marry me. He knew me inside and out. Better than any psychiatrist He knew me. My Father not only knew what I was like right then but He also knew what I would be like fifteen years later. How could a psychiatrist know me that well? My own mother couldn't know me that well! But God my Father did. And He gave me Gloria. He provided for my need. I needed her to love me, to understand me, to keep me straight, to make me humble, to make me happy, to make me a real man!

My Father is not a nickel-and-dime father. He is not concerned only with my financial needs. He provides for His children, and that includes bringing the right people into their lives.

Many times we have needed people to work in various areas of the Outreach for Youth ministry which I sponsor. God has always sent the right person along, just at the right time! There have been times in my personal life that I have been in great need of fellowship, of friendship, of someone simply to talk with and be close to and share things with. And always my Father has seen that need and sent that person my way. There have been times that I have needed someone to rebuke me in a spirit of love, to speak to me a word of warning or prophecy from the Lord, and God has always provided that person just when I needed him most.

God is good. And sometimes it seems that He has been especially good to me. He found me on the streets of New York City. I was full of bitterness and evil. I hated God. I hated people. Most of all I hated Nicky Cruz. I didn't find God; God found me. How He loved me enough to be looking for me is a wonder and a miracle, but somehow He did. He saved me, cleaned me up, pulled me off the streets, and gave me a ministry. He gave me a beautiful wife and a family. He gave me friends and a comfortable home.

Sometimes I am asked, "Why you, Nicky? Why are you where you are now, when so many others are still on the street, still hooked, still in sin?" And I ask myself that question sometimes. I ask why I am here when so many of my old gang are in jail or the hospital or the grave.

Is it because the Father loves me more than He loves them? No, a thousand times, no! God loves every man the same. But it is up to every man how deeply he is willing to go into that love, how much he is willing to trust it, how completely he will lie back and rest in the arms of a loving Father. I had gone so low in sin that I was willing to be a fool for Jesus. I wanted a heavenly Father so badly that I was willing to plunge deeply into His love. I held nothing back because I had nothing to lose. I had nothing to live for but the love of my new Father.

And even today, when it seems that God is not providing for me as He should, I remind myself that it is not God who stops giving. It is Nicky Cruz who stops receiving. God the Father provides for all His children, but some are willing to go more deeply into His daily love than others are.

If it seems that God does not provide for you, perhaps it is you who makes the difference. It is not that God does not want to bless His children. It is that we put Him into a box. We expect nothing from Him and we get it. We think we are big now, we are grown-up now, we can do it all without Daddy now. We are smart enough to run things by ourselves now.

That is so dumb. We need to work harder at being God's little children instead of trying to be big shots all the time. We need to crawl up into our Father's lap, like a child, and say, "Here I am, Father. I am Nicky Cruz, Your little boy. You know what I need better than I know, so give it to me and I will take it and do something to make You proud of me!"

When a child is willing to be a child, a father cannot help but become the best father he knows how to be. And God knows how to be the best Father of all.

THE
MAGNIFICENT
HOLY SPIRIT

11

Where the Healing Begins

There are bad people in the world—bad, hurting people, because sin has made them that way. They are bad as a festering sore is bad, full of pus and poison and oozing with pain that you can almost see, bad to feel and bad to touch, bad even to look at. There are people in the world who are like that. They are in the prisons and on the streets. They are in the big, frantic cities and the small, decaying towns. They may look dirty and poor or slick and proud. But they are all alike on the inside, full of hurting pain and bitterness, full of sin that eats like acid inside them and turns their food to ashes in their mouths.

I have seen them and once I was one of them. I know what it is to look in the mirror and hate what I see. I know what it is to feel a hurting inside that won't go away, not even at night, a hurting so bad that it turned my dreams into nightmares. I was one of those walking sores, a solid piece of hatred five feet seven inches tall, just looking for someone to push and shove and hurt because I hurt so much myself. It has been many years since I was on the street, but still I see them there by the hundreds of thousands, black and white and in-between, painted females and strutting males, young and full of nerves and energy or old and tired and almost dead.

There are bad people in the world, and not all the psychiatrists and social workers in the country can even crack the door that will release them from their prison of misery.

Every bad man, deep in his heart, wants to have peace. He is looking for peace in his heart, and he doesn't know how to find it. He doesn't know how to get it. So he strikes out. He becomes bitter and full of hatred. He feels that whatever he does is wrong—that he is going to be put down for it, busted for it, that there is a bird flying over his head all the time dumping on him. Nothing he does can change that. So he turns mean; he puts on a bad face; he becomes aggressive and hostile. But inside he is just a little boy who wants love in his heart. He wants peace in his life. He wants to drain all the bitterness and the hurt out of himself.

How can such a man be touched by God? God the Father is just another cop, another jailer, another symbol of authority from which he is running. God the

Saviour is a faraway, abstract Jesus in a white robe riding a donkey. How does the junkie, the rapist, the wino
with vomit on his shirt, the angry, bitter black man
ever reach the point of opening himself to the healing
power of Jesus or the strong love of God the Father?

Enter the Holy Spirit. The soothing, softening,
gentling Holy Spirit of God. It is the Holy Spirit who
calms the beast in a man, the Holy Spirit who banishes
the anger and the hatred, drains off the bitterness and
the pain, takes the blinders off and lets him see a loving
God rather than a fearsome, frightening one. The Holy
Spirit lets him see Jesus for what He is, and somehow,
miraculously, the healing process begins.

12

The Fuel That Keeps Us Going

God is a magnificent Father.

God is a magnificent Saviour, Jesus Christ.

But if it were not for the magnificent Holy Spirit, I would still be a wretched, hateful sinner!

It is not enough to have a Father-God who loves and provides for me. It is not enough even to have a Saviour who died for my sins. For any of those blessings to make a difference in our lives, there must also be present in this world that Third Person of God, the Holy Spirit.

It is amazing to me how many people regard the Holy Spirit as a second-rate afterthought when they think about God. They give Him shabby treatment, as if He were not really quite as important as the Father and the Son. They throw Him in as an afterthought, like this: "Praise God! Thank You, Jesus! And, oh, yes, I appreciate You, too, Holy Spirit, whatever You are." The fact is that the Holy Spirit is fully as necessary and important to you and me as Jesus Christ is. Without Him we would all be lost.

You say, "But isn't it Jesus Christ who died for me? And isn't it God the Father who forgives me of sin?"

Yes, it is. But why did you come to Jesus in the first place? Because you were drawn by God the Holy Spirit. Why did you confess your sins? Because the Holy Spirit convicted you of those sins. He made you feel guilty and unclean. He showed you the filthiness of your flesh and your need of a Saviour. And how were you able to see and believe that Jesus was God? By the power of the Holy Spirit, who miraculously lifted the scales from your blind, natural eyes and let you see with spiritual eyes the hope of Jesus.

Jesus saved me; the Father forgave me. But the Holy Spirit convicted me, brought me to my knees, and showed me God. Without Him I would still be full of sin, and I wouldn't even know it! I would still be frustrated and bitter, and I wouldn't even know why! But the Holy Spirit grabbed me by my shoulders, shook me hard, and pulled away the screen of the flesh that kept me from seeing the things of the Spirit. He showed me my sin, and I was crushed by its black, awful weight. He showed me Jesus Christ, and I was gripped by His strong, sweet love. And then He shoved me toward God, and I gladly fell into the arms of my loving Father.

What a magnificent Holy Spirit!

And after I became a Christian, the Holy Spirit was not finished with me. Every day of my life, He is the fuel that keeps me going. He is like gasoline in an automobile. A forty-thousand-dollar Rolls Royce is much more impressive than a sixty-cent gallon of gas. But the Rolls Royce without the gasoline in it is useless. It is just a forty-thousand-dollar hunk of steel. It will not take anybody anywhere. But when you pour that gasoline into the car, suddenly all the magnificence of that fantastic machine comes to life, and will take you wherever you need to go in style, speed, and comfort.

The Holy Spirit is like that. All the might of the Father and all the love of the Son are useless to me unless I can see them and believe in them. The Holy Spirit gives me the power to do that. How can a child of the flesh see the things of God? Only by the help of the Spirit!

Even the Bible depends on the Holy Spirit. Without Him, the Bible is just paper and ink to me. It is just another book. It is full of big words and difficult language. It is beyond me. It talks of things which I cannot understand, so how can it show me the great and mysterious things of God? Through the Holy Spirit! I open my Bible, and the Holy Spirit comes to my mind and illuminates the Word of God so that it leaps off the page at me and talks to me. My mind is like a room that is dark and gloomy because heavy, thick curtains cover the windows. But as I read the Scripture, the Holy Spirit reaches with a giant hand and rips the curtains off the wall, and the sunlight pours through the window and fills the room with bright light. With one mighty stroke the Spirit illuminates the Bible, and it fills me up with God's words and wisdom.

My preaching and my writing depend totally on the Holy Spirit. If He is not there with me, anointing me, nothing happens. Nothing. I feel nothing, I say nothing, I accomplish nothing. I will confess that I have had these times. I have been in the pulpit with only the flesh and not the Spirit. It gives me a sick feeling, a weak feeling. I have to face it in prayer. I implore the Father to send the Spirit to fill me up and flow through me, to unlock my heart and let my feelings run out to the people, to touch my lips and make them speak the things of God. And the Spirit comes, and when He does the presence of Jesus Christ is so real, the power of God is released. I preach and it is as if the heavens are ringing out the truth of God. I feel more deeply. I love more strongly. My compassion grows and multiplies. And people are drawn to the altar to confront Jesus for themselves.

Why do so many people ignore this magnificent God? Why do they love the Father and the Saviour so much and think so little of the Holy Spirit? Maybe it is because the Pentecostals and the charismatics have taught so strongly about the gifts of the Spirit that we forget sometimes that He is more than all that. He does more than bring the supernatural gifts. He does more than enable us to speak in tongues.

I believe in speaking in unknown tongues and I believe in the gifts of the Spirit. I am grateful to the

Holy Spirit for the miracles which He brings to us. But tongues and the gifts are only a small part of what the Holy Spirit means in my life, and I don't want ever to become so carried away with those things that I forget to love the Spirit for *all* that He is. In the total view of the relationship of God and man, speaking in tongues is a rather small thing. It is certainly not worth fighting over, not worth all the splits and schisms and fusses that have erupted over it. I have many wonderful Christian brothers and sisters who have never spoken in tongues, but whose lives constantly show the presence of the Holy Spirit. God doesn't want me to fuss with them over that, or them with me.

Let God take care of those things. Let the Holy Spirit reveal Himself in whatever way He chooses to whomever He chooses. Why all the arguing over it? If a Christian brother tells me he has been baptized with the Holy Spirit and has never spoken in tongues, I say, "Praise the Lord, brother," and go on doing God's work. If another brother tells me he speaks in tongues every day, I say, "Praise the Lord, brother," and go on doing God's work.

God is a God of the supernatural. Of course He is! And the Holy Spirit is the person of God who prepares us earthly, human creatures to understand and receive the supernatural things of God. It is the Holy Spirit who opens us up to the supernatural. And just as some Christians are hung up on tongues and gifts and miracles, others are so prejudiced against those things that they live like spiritual dwarfs, always thinking about

God but never feeling Him, always talking about God's power but never seeing it at work.

God wants to open you up to the supernatural; and for that to happen, you must give the magnificent Holy Spirit a place in your heart that is fully equal to that of the Father and the Son.

Listen to the Spirit! You listen to the Father as He promises to provide for you. You listen to the Son as He forgives your sins. Now listen to the Holy Spirit as He pushes you out into the supernatural! Let Him turn you on to possibility of miracles in your life! Let Him open you up to the supernatural power of God in you! If you will give Him a chance, the Holy Spirit can take your human reasoning, your intellect, your logical mind, and charge it all with the electricity of the supernatural. That is what He can do if you let Him!

When I talk about supernatural things happening in your life, do you automatically think about healings and miracles and signs?

If you do, don't!

The fruits of the Holy Spirit are just as super-natural as the gifts. It is easy to look at a healing or a miracle and say, "Oh, wow, how supernatural that is!" But what about love? What about peace? What about joy? Those things are supernatural, too. They are just as miraculous—if they are genuinely a part of a person's life—as the healing of a broken leg.

The fruits of the Holy Spirit, according to the Bible, are love, joy, peace, long-suffering, gentleness, goodness, faith, meekness, and temperance (*see* Galatians 5:22, 23).

What a list of supernatural qualities! In this world of greed and selfishness, when "dog eat dog" describes the way most men behave, the presence of true love in a man's heart, the kind of love that includes even his enemies, is a supernatural love! It is a miracle! It is not natural for me to be loving toward those who hate me. It is natural for me to hate them back. But the love that the Spirit gives me for them is supernatural!

Is it natural to have joy and peace in a world like the one we live in, with everything caving in around us and our whole society coming unglued? Of course not! The natural thing to do is to look at all the trouble in the world, sit down in the middle of the floor, and cry like a baby. But the Holy Spirit gives joy and peace, a supernatural joy and peace that is a miracle of God. It doesn't make sense. It isn't rational. But it is there—the peace of the Spirit in the middle of a rotten, dying world!

That is the way with all the fruits of the Spirit: they are supernatural and they come from God Almighty. We don't manufacture them. We don't work them up from our own flesh. God the Holy Spirit puts them into us supernaturally, and that is a miracle as great as any that ever occurs in a healing campaign.

For a long time I did not understand that. I thought God expected me to produce these fruits by myself. I thought I had to love my enemies, keep peace and joy in my heart, be long-suffering in all kinds of trouble, and all the rest—strictly on my own! *That's impossible!* I thought. And I was right. I constantly fell short of what I thought God wanted, and that made me feel guilty.

I'll never forget one Christmas, early in my ministry, when Gloria and I were supporting a center for home-less street kids in Los Angeles. We had taken all our money to buy an old house for the center. When Christ-mas Eve came, we had no money for gifts for the kids, a special Christmas meal, or anything else. We scraped together all the money we could find—thirty-seven dollars—and bought pork chops for all the kids with a few sacks of groceries to go along with them. We spent every dime and had Christmas dinner with those kids and those pork chops. I watched them eat so hungrily and felt such sadness for them that their Christmas could not be bigger and better.

That day I began to feel sorry for them and sorry for myself. And the self-pity turned quickly to bitter-ness. I remember driving around Los Angeles that day, looking at all those big, beautiful, million-dollar churches, and thinking about all the money that was spent to make them more beautiful, to build them bigger, while we were so in need, almost starving with our house full of boys and that pitiful little pan of pork chops. It was hard for me to love those middle-class Christians that day—hard for me to feel that joy, to have that long-suffering that Scripture talks about.

And I felt guilty. This is not the way of God, I thought. This bitterness, this anger, this is not the way I should feel. God had to teach me a lesson. He had to teach me that I do not manufacture this supernatural love. I do not make it up. God the Holy Spirit gives it to me as I ask Him to do so. He sends it into my heart.

God would not expect me to heal a man's broken leg by my own power. He would not say, *You are a Christian now, Nicky, so you should be able to heal this man.* Of course not! But *He* will heal the man in answer to my prayer. He doesn't expect me to do the work but only to allow the Spirit to do it through me. And the supernatural love, the supernatural joy and peace, the supernatural gentleness and goodness—all are put into my life by the magnificent Holy Spirit.

Oh, blessed Holy Spirit God, open me up to Your presence every day that I live! When my feet hit the floor every morning, let me be open to You that day. Thank You, Father, for loving me. Thank You, Saviour, for forgiving me. And thank You, Holy Spirit, for filling me and walking with me every day!

13

The "Power Trap"

There are ways to abuse the Holy Spirit, ways of using His power for the wrong purposes. Some people have the wrong idea about why the Spirit is here. They see the great miracles, the fantastic things that are done by the Holy Spirit, and they are carried away by the glamour and excitement of it all. I have met people in the charismatic movement who have absolutely no patience with anything that is not flashy or spectacular. They have become obsessed with power and have no time for the less dramatic things which the Holy Spirit does.

This problem is not a new one. In the New Testament, the man whom we remember as Simon the Sorcerer was obsessed with the power that the Holy Spirit brought to the Christians of that day. He misunderstood it completely. He thought it was a thing that could be bought and sold. He looked at the power of the Holy Spirit as something like the power of electricity, that can be turned on and off by whoever owns the electric machine.

Simon thought the Holy Spirit was a thing, a trick to be mastered, an object that he could own. So he tried to buy the Holy Spirit! He clearly did not think of the Holy Spirit as God, not as the magnificent person of the eternal God, but as a power source, like a gasoline engine or a genie in a bottle from some magic fairy tale. How stupid of him to want to *buy* God Almighty! How totally stupid to think of the Holy Spirit as a thing that the apostles "had" and which they could therefore give to him!

The apostles did not "have" the Holy Spirit; the Holy Spirit had them! They did not own the power that seemed always to be present with them; the magnificent Holy Spirit was side by side with them, and He had all the power of heaven and earth because He was God Almighty.

It is easy enough to talk about the stupidity of Simon the Sorcerer, but some people today are no better. They behave as stupidly as Simon did, and they are Christians and should know better! They treat the Holy Spirit as a "thing," a power source to be used for their own glory. They talk about "having" the Holy Spirit as if they owned it.

The Holy Spirit is not a thing!

The Holy Spirit cannot be owned by any man!

The Holy Spirit is more than a source of power!

The Holy Spirit is not simply a name to call on for miracles and wonders and spectacular healings!

The Holy Spirit is God. He is a personal being who wishes to interact with us personally, to communicate with us in rich and personal ways, not to be used by us as an object, a giant battery in the sky that charges us with power at the flip of a switch and is ignored the rest of the time. He does not wish to be taken out of a box, called upon to produce great healings and great miracles, then put back into the box until it is time to perform again.

But some people become so obsessed with power that they think of little else; to them the Holy Spirit becomes the source of power and nothing more. I believe in the power of God to heal and work miracles. But I would not be honest if I did not admit that this preoccupation is a temptation into which we who are charismatic believers can easily fall. It is easy for a person to see God's power and be so zonked by it that it gets out of perspective.

Take me, for instance.

I fell into the "power trap" when I was a young man at the Bible Institute in California. I was fresh off the streets of New York with no grounding in the Scriptures. I had seen healings. I had seen evil men brought to tears in a moment's time by the Spirit of God. I had seen miracles performed in answer to prayer. And, more than anything in the world, I wanted to have the power of the Holy Spirit in my life as I had seen it in the lives of others. I wanted to heal the sick, perform miracles, bring hardened sinners to their knees.

So I prayed, "Oh, God, make me a more powerful Nicky Cruz!" I did not ask God for more love for the lost, for a clearer vision of Jesus, for a more compassionate heart, for a sharper sensitivity to the will of God. I prayed only for power!

I had no concept of the Holy Spirit as my teacher, my guide, my comfort in times of sorrow. I thought of the Holy Spirit as "something," not as "someone." I thought of the Holy Spirit as a thing that, if I prayed hard enough, God would give to me to make me more powerful. I did not think of Him as a magnificent God-Person whom I could know and love as I knew and loved Jesus Himself.

I was sincere. I prayed long hours for the power that I wanted God to give me in the form of the Holy Spirit. When I still did not see great power in my life, I decided to fast. If I fasted enough, I figured, God would be forced to give me power as a reward for my fasting. So I fasted and prayed as seriously as anyone ever did. But I was doing it with the wrong attitude and for the wrong reasons.

God taught me a lesson. I was in a period of heavy fasting and prayer one day and I was obsessed with this idea of being powerful in the Holy Spirit. I prayed, "Oh, Lord, make me a powerful man of God." And as I prayed, I had a mental picture of myself in the pulpit preaching, with people being healed and saved, and people jumping around and shouting and saying, "Oh, what a powerful man of God is Nicky Cruz!"

I took a break from my session of prayer and went for a walk to clear my head and get some fresh air. I was just saturated with the idea of the power of the Holy Spirit. As I was walking past a building with a brick surface, I stopped on the sidewalk and said, "God, now that I am so close with You, I am going to show You that I can hit my fist through this wall and not hurt it!" That sounds ridiculous, but it is exactly what I was thinking. I was on such a superspiritual binge that I thought I could drive my fist through that brick wall without hurting it, just from the sheer power of God in me.

So I doubled up my fist, drew back, and pounded it into that brick wall as hard as I could. You can guess what happened. The wall didn't budge. I yelped with pain and pulled back a bloody, bruised fist. I hurt my fist so badly I almost cried.

My immediate reaction was to be hurt with God. I felt that He had let me down. I had so much faith in the Holy Spirit, and He wouldn't even give me enough power to bust up a few bricks! I was hurt with God because He didn't act according to the Gospel of Nicky Cruz! I had the idea that if I prayed and fasted enough, I had a free ticket to whatever I wanted from God, no matter how silly it was. But God does not act that way. He is not a little puppy dog who follows us around and does tricks for us whenever we say the magic words.

The Holy Spirit taught me a lesson that day. He

taught me a new respect for Himself. He taught me a new humility. I stood there holding a bleeding hand and the Holy Spirit let me see how silly I was. God teaches some lessons the simple, hard way. That's the way it was with me. He taught me to humble myself and not worry so much about power. God was not interested in my running around showing off, and I had a bruised, painful hand for the next few days to remind me of that!

I still want to be a man of power with God. I still want to see people healed and touched by the Holy Spirit. But I realize now that there are many things more important than how powerful I appear to be.

14

The Voice of
the Spirit

I grew up in the streets.

Almost literally, it was in the streets that I grew
from a boy into a man. The streets were my education;
the ghetto was my only Sunday school. I was born in
Puerto Rico, one of eighteen children of a man who
made a living in black magic and a woman who was
known throughout the village as a witch. At the age of
fifteen I was shipped to New York City to live with an
older brother.

In only a few months I left my brother's home, quit
school, and lived in the streets and back alleys of Brooklyn. It was the Brooklyn of the 1950s, and street gangs
were a fact of life. You joined a gang or you lived with
constant harassment and fear of much worse. I joined a

gang. The name of the group was the Mau Maus, and I became its president after a few months. I learned the ways of the switchblade knife, the bicycle chain, and the sawed-off shotgun. I learned the ways of winos, pimps, hookers, and potheads. I learned the ways of street fights, all-night beer busts, and loose-and-easy sex.

I never learned the ways of civilized, wholesome people. And I certainly never learned the ways of God.

Then I met Jesus Christ. I met Him on the street because that was where I lived. If it had been necessary for me to go to a beautiful cathedral with golden altars and stained-glass windows to meet Jesus, I would never have met Him. I lived on the street, and that is where Jesus Christ came to confront me. He came to me through the message of a preacher who dared to invade my turf, who endured the catcalls and the jeers and threats to bring Jesus Christ to the streets of Brooklyn. I literally slapped that preacher in the face, just to express my contempt for what he was doing, but Jesus put a hook in my heart that day. I couldn't shake it loose and I couldn't forget what I had heard. A few days later, I knelt in a prayer room at the Saint Nicholas Arena and accepted Jesus Christ as my Saviour. He forgave my sins and made me His son.

But I was still a product of the streets.

God didn't take the top off my head and pour the knowledge of His Word in! He washed my heart clean, but my head was still empty of the principles of Christian living. All I knew was that I was now a disciple of Jesus Christ, that I should read my Bible and pray every

day, and that I should quit fighting my enemies and
trying to chop their heads off! Brother Dave Wilkerson
told me that right away! But that was all I knew—except
that I had a wonderful peace and feeling of love inside
me that I wanted never to lose.

I had a girl friend whose name was Lydia. She was
a beautiful girl and I liked her very much. We had been
sleeping together for several months, and neither of us
thought of it as something that was wrong or sinful.
It wasn't illegal. It didn't hurt anybody, as a .38 revolver
or a knife did. We were in love, so we had sex. That
seemed perfectly natural to me, and when I went home
after becoming a Christian it never even occurred to me
that God wanted me to stop sleeping with my girl friend.
To people who have grown up around the church, that
may sound impossible, but it is true! I had never heard
of sex being considered wrong if both people agreed
to it.

Lydia became a Christian at the Saint Nicholas
Arena the same night I did, so for the next four nights
after our conversion experience, we went back home
and went to bed together. We read the Bible to each
other, prayed, and went to bed. But on the fifth night
something was different. I read a chapter of the Bible
to her, then she read a chapter to me, and then we got
into bed.

And suddenly I felt a terrible sadness. It was a
strange emotion, one I had never felt before. It was a
heavy sadness. I didn't feel good; I didn't feel clean. I

had a terrible feeling that something was wrong. I didn't want to touch Lydia. I didn't want to caress her.

"What's the matter?" she asked.

"I don't know, Lydia, but something is wrong. There is something about what we are doing that is wrong. I should feel happy, but I feel sad. What we are doing is bad. Somehow it's not right. I've got to talk to a preacher and find out what's happening with me."

"But Nicky, it's two o'clock in the morning! You can't go see a preacher now!"

"Okay," I said. "I'll wait till morning. But I'm going to get somebody to explain this to me."

So all night long I didn't touch her. I didn't sleep very much, either. I tossed and turned, waiting for morning.

At six o'clock I could wait no longer. I jumped out of bed and dashed down the street several blocks to the home of Luis Arce, the pastor of a little Spanish-speaking church in Brooklyn. I whammed on the door. No answer. I whammed on it again, harder this time. Finally Brother Arce pushed open the door, rubbing his eyes.

"Brother Arce, I've got to talk to you!" I blurted.

"Nicky! Do you know what time it is?" Then he shrugged and smiled, opening the door wider and gesturing me inside. "You know I'm always ready to talk with you, Nicky. Come on in."

I told him about what Lydia and I were doing, and how that night I had felt such a terrible sadness, a feeling of shame and wrong. "Why do I feel this way,

Brother Arce?" I asked him. "I got to know if something
I'm doing is making me feel this way."

He pulled his Bible off the shelf and began to look
for a particular passage. When he found it he paused,
looked up at me, and said, "Nicky, what you are doing
is called 'fornication.' "

"Fornication?" I had never heard the word. "What
is fornication?"

"Nicky," he told me quietly, "fornication is shack-
ing up. The Bible calls it fornication. And it is wrong,
Nicky. It is sinful, and it hurts Jesus when you do it.
That is why you feel so bad. The Holy Spirit has given
you a bad feeling to stop you." And he showed me verse
after verse in the Bible that speaks of the sinfulness of
fornication. Before I left there, I had cried before God.
I had asked for His forgiveness for my sin. And the sadness had lifted.

That was a beautiful experience. It was my first real
contact with the Holy Spirit as a separate and distinct
person of the Magnificent Three. Jesus Christ had saved
me and become my Saviour-God. The Father had
adopted me and become my Father-God. And now I
learned for the first time of the powerful ministry of
God the Holy Spirit—the ministry of guiding me, direct-
ing me toward what I needed to know and do.

There have been dozens of times since then that the
Holy Spirit has shown me the way to go, but never with
more clarity and force than in that first week of my new
life. He showed me how to please Jesus Christ better.
He showed me sin in my life that I was not aware of. He

did a job on my soul like the job an X-ray machine does on my body. He showed me a bad spot on the inside that I could not see with my own eyes, so that I could do something about it. I don't ever need to worry about doing something sinful and being unaware of it—not so long as I am listening to the Holy Spirit. If I am sensitive to the Spirit, He will always steer me away from sin; if I start down the wrong path, He will stop me with a flashing red light in my heart.

My conscience cannot always be depended on. Sometimes it goes to sleep. Sometimes I can slip a sin past it, do something wrong without my conscience feeling bad. Maybe it is because my conscience is hardened. Maybe it is because I have been taught improperly, or not taught at all. It would be dangerous for me to say, "Well, this thing I am doing must be okay because it doesn't hurt my conscience to do it."

My human reasoning cannot be relied on to show me right from wrong, either. Too many people have figured out with their brains what is right and what is wrong, and human reasoning is what they live by. But heads can be screwed on wrong sometimes. Human reasoning can become twisted and bent out of shape. Your brain can tell you a lie if you want it to tell you one. The Bible says, "There is a way which seemeth right unto a man, but the end thereof are the ways of death" (Proverbs 14:12). That Scripture gives me a chill. It frightens me. It tells me that if I depend on my head alone, I may miss the truth.

And I cannot depend on other people, either. Ten

preachers might tell me ten different things. Preacher A says, "Do it"; Preacher B says, "Don't do it." This church reads a Scripture verse and tells me it means one thing; that church reads the same verse and tells me the opposite. People have been messing other people up since New Testament days. The Bible calls it the blind leading the blind (*see* Matthew 15:14). It is foolish and dangerous for me to listen to one church—any church—or one man—any man—and live my life by what he says.

So what can I do to know how to please God my Father? How can I be sure I am a good disciple of Jesus Christ my Saviour?

Enter the magnificent Holy Spirit!

He shows me the way. He does for me what the pillars of smoke and fire did for the wandering Hebrew children. He tells me when to stay and when to go. If I know Him and love Him, if I listen to His voice, He will not let me drift into sin because of a hardened conscience, or because of a confused mind, or because of a misguided minister. He will prod me constantly toward what is best for me as a child of God. He will take me as far into the things of God as I am willing to go. He helps me to grow up. He brings me along at my own best pace, gradually weaning me from the milk of the Christian life and giving me a diet of meat. He makes the Father's love real to me. He makes the Saviour's presence real to me. He makes the supernatural quality of the Holy Bible real to me. He takes my fearful, blind human nature and changes me into someone who can see God and hear His voice.

Looking over the years of my Christian walk, I can see certain decisions which stand out as crucial ones, decisions that changed the course of my life. In every case the Holy Spirit helped to guide me. In every case I would have made the wrong move without Him.

After I was saved, I spent three years at the La Puente Bible Institute in California, then moved back to New York with Gloria, my bride, to work with Dave Wilkerson as one of the leaders of the Teen Challenge Center there. That decision was of God, I am convinced. I had many invitations to go here or there to work for the Lord. I couldn't feel strongly that any of them were right for me. I was uncertain about whether I should begin an evangelistic pulpit ministry immediately or work with drug addicts, or what.

One of the ministers at the Bible Institute challenged me to pray that God would cause the next letter I received to be from the person or work that I should go to. I prayed about it and it seemed the right thing to do. I committed myself in prayer to accept the very next invitation which came in the mail, regardless of what it was. The Holy Spirit gave me peace about that commitment. A day or so later the mail came, and with it a letter from Dave Wilkerson in New York. I hadn't heard from him in months. "Come back to New York and help us in the center. We need you," he said. That was all I needed. One week earlier I would have said no to that letter without even considering it. But I had committed my decision to the Holy Spirit, and I knew that it was not Dave Wilkerson but the Holy Spirit talking in that letter. I went to New York and God blessed me there.

A few years later I left Teen Challenge because I felt that my work there was over. Once again I felt that the Holy Spirit had led me, this time back to the West Coast. I knew I had done the right thing, but as the weeks passed I began to wonder, to second-guess myself, to fear that I had made the wrong move. I was living in Oakland, waiting for some guidance from God. Nothing came and I began to get frustrated and bitter. It seemed that God was slamming doors in my face. I flew back to New York to talk to Dave Wilkerson about starting a center for addicts in the Bronx, but he didn't feel that it was a good thing to do. I returned to Oakland, and things got tighter as the weeks dragged by. I had a heavy heart. I was hurt with God for leading me all the way to the West Coast and not opening something up for me right away.

Our money had run out. We had almost no food in the house. I began to get desperate and decided it was time for me to take matters into my own hands. I was tired of waiting for God to move. So I started looking for a job, any job. But God closed the door. Nobody would hire me. I began to think it was because I was Puerto Rican, so I tried for the jobs that I thought even a prejudiced man would give me—washing dishes, working in a cannery, packing meat in a plant, anything. It did no good. Gloria started looking for jobs. Same story. If there were ten of us in a particular employment office, the other nine would get jobs, but not Gloria or me. The Holy Spirit was closing the doors. I was discouraged.

Then it happened. A call came from a youth crusade in Oakland. Could I come and preach a service? Could I? Can a bird fly? Is grass green? I preached that night and, though I was personally at a low ebb spiritually, the Holy Spirit fell over the congregation and people were saved. I was so happy that I took the small cash offering they gave me that night and drove downtown toward a favorite restaurant, intending to take Gloria out to eat. As I began to make a right-hand turn off the main street, something came over me suddenly and I made a sharp, tire-screeching U-turn instead, heading back the other way.

I felt the Holy Spirit telling me to pray. I drove straight to our ramshackle little apartment, fell on my knees, and emptied out my heart and soul to my heavenly Father. I poured out all the hurt and frustration. I emptied all the bitterness and confusion. I cried like a hungry baby. I soaked up the sweet presence of the Holy Spirit. For four hours Gloria and I prayed, and the Holy Spirit spoke through Gloria in a prophecy: *This is the day that the Lord has heard you. I will bless you as you preach My Word. I will take you and use you to reach young people.* It was a confirmation of an earlier prophecy, made long ago at the Bible Institute, and it broke me and shook me and pushed me into the arms of God.

After that night, invitations began to come in from all over California, and soon from across the country, to preach. I moved out for God. My ability to speak

English improved. I gained confidence in the pulpit. The Holy Spirit, having pushed me out of the nest, taught me to fly! And until this day I have preached the Gospel all over the world. How easily I could have missed it! Can you imagine what might have happened if one of those Oakland restaurants had needed a good Puerto Rican dishwasher?

But God would not let it happen. The Holy Spirit, the magnificent, guiding Spirit of God, led me all the way!